# Acknowledgements

This publication would not have been possible without the contributions of many. I particularly wish to thank Barbara Western, Brian Gumm, Paula Shoecraft, Sam Kim and Gary Bass at OMB Watch. Without their help, this publication would not have seen the light of day.

Equally important are the many advocates, elected officials, students, and ordinary citizens from around the nation with whom I have had the privilege to work, and whose stories are at the hearts of this publication. Special thanks go to each of you.

This new edition of *So You Want to Make a Difference* is one product of the Civic Engagement Project (CEP), a joint effort with OMB Watch. CEP focuses on increasing the capacity of nonprofit groups to engage in public policy advocacy. CEP offers trainings, consultation, user-friendly tools, and publications for effective public policy advocacy.

I look forward to our next advocacy adventures together.

**Nancy Amidei**
Civic Engagement Project
Seattle, WA 98105
(206) 528-1653

---

## ABOUT OMB WATCH

OMB Watch is a nonprofit government watchdog organization dedicated to promoting government accountability, citizen participation in public policy decisions, and the use of fiscal and regulatory policy to serve the public interest.

OMB Watch
1742 Connecticut Ave NW
Washington, DC 20009
(202) 234-8494 (phone)
(202) 234-8584 (fax)
www.ombwatch.org
ombwatch@ombwatch.org

# Understanding Butter

Here is a classic political story.

Once upon a time, there was a fellow who was newly elected to the United State Senate. He was so pleased with himself after his election that the first time someone invited him to a fancy banquet... he showed up early.

In fact, he was so early he was practically the only one in the big banquet hall. The only other person was the waitress, and she was doing her job: she was putting out the butter.

Nothing else was going on so he watched her, and she went methodically about her work. Every time she saw a plate, she put a pat of butter. Around the room she went: one plate, one pat of butter... one plate, one pat of butter... one plate, one pat of butter.

Finally she got to him. Giving her his best, most winning smile he said, "I really like butter. Think I could have another pat of butter?"

"Sorry sir," she said. "I treat everyone the same: one plate gets one pat of butter."

She went on about her work.

He was not pleased (that is the polite version). He sat there for a minute, thinking about this, but when he looked around the room there was still hardly anyone in the place. So he got up and he followed her – she was working on another table by now.

"Hhummph," he said, clearing his throat and looking straight at her, "maybe you do not know who I am – I'm a United States Senator!"

"Maybe you do not know who *I* am," she replied. "*I'm* the one who gives out the butter."

The moral of this story is that Votes are like Butter – and we are the ones who give out the Butter! As citizens, we have something every candidate and every elected official wants, from school board to President: they want our butter. They want a cholesterol hit!

Every time we shake an elected official's hand and say where we live ("Hi, I'm Nancy A. and I live in your District") they hear a little voice saying: "butter." If we mention belonging to a group with a few dozen people in the District, that little voice says: "butter butter." And if we can identify with a coalition of organizations representing hundreds (or thousands!) of voters, that little voice turns into a veritable roar!

Ask elected officials which is more important to them, money... or votes... and the answer is always the same: votes. The reason is also the same: they can always go outside of the District (where their voters live) for money, but they can never go outside the District for votes. To get and stay in office, they have to win over 51% of the people with the butter. That is us – which is why each of us can be so powerful.

# Table of Contents

# Introduction

Welcome to policy advocacy. If you have ever spoken up on behalf of someone you cared about, then you have been an advocate. It is that simple.

There is a mystique surrounding advocacy – that you have to be an expert on your issue, or an expert in the way the process works. Not so. It is true that some kinds of advocacy require considerable knowledge and expertise, but advocacy is like anything else: beginners are not expected to know as much as professionals, and the more you do it, the easier it gets.

Even lobbying a legislator can be easy. All you have to do is develop a clear, simple message (a problem to call attention to, some useful personal experience, a proposal that you would like to see enacted or rejected), and deliver it. That is it. If you can do that, you can be a policy advocate.

This manual is designed to give you some of the details you will need along the way, and ways to find more sophisticated help and information as they are needed.

***So You Want to Make a Difference* was written with three goals in mind:**

- To help citizens feel more confident about getting involved in policy advocacy;

- To equip local leaders with some tools so they can teach others about policy advocacy;

- To stimulate involvement in democratic decision-making and provide information about key resources.

Throughout, the examples provided will show the importance of getting involved, and how ordinary people can make a difference. (By now this manual has been through 13 printings.)

The Butter Story is at the heart of what public policy advocacy is all about. It is true that there are some complicated aspects to policy-making, and more details than any one person can ever master. It is also true that some people have to be on hand with expert knowledge of the subject, the bills, and the process. But most of us just have to understand the power of the "butter:" that as citizens and voters we have a voice in the decisions that affect our lives. If we organize enough butter – 51% – we can make a difference. Just taking part in working toward that 51% can be a powerful experience.

To some the word "advocacy" conjures up visions of mass demonstrations and public protests, or well-paid lobbyists in expensive suits. But a lot of advocacy is just a matter of seeing a need and finding a way to address it. It means literally "to plead the cause of another" – which most of us do all the time on behalf of our neighbors, our families, our friends. Policy advocacy is the next logical step. It carries that pleading into the political arena, and does it on behalf of people we may not know personally. It is a practical way to translate basic values like respect for human dignity or concern for the environment into policies and laws, and it is a core part of our American democracy.

Plenty of good people are eager to be involved in working for stronger communities and a better future, but unsure how to go about it. Lots of people know they should be more involved, but cannot think how to find the time in already busy lives. Still others are those who, for one reason or another, sit on the sidelines while some people suffer – but want to act. All of these are the people for whom this was written.

## HOW TO USE THIS MANUAL

Since much of the material that follows is information most people know but just have not thought about lately, in many ways it is like a refresher course. Much of advocacy is like that. It depends less on material found in books, and more on lessons learned in the process of living: how power is wielded, how people are motivated, and how those with power are influenced. In short, it is about how government works and social change is won.

Throughout, that newly remembered knowledge will be applied to the idea of winning better laws and policies on behalf of vulnerable people and causes in local communities everywhere.

Think of it as a kind of road map, a guide through:

- Policy Advocacy;

- Our system of government;

- Practical ideas for getting started;

- Some of the "nuts and bolts" of advocacy; and

- Additional benefits advocacy can provide.

## WHO SHOULD USE THIS MANUAL?

Individuals will find many useful ideas in the material that follows. It gives concrete examples; offers useful advice; and provides valuable basic information about how public policies get made.

However working in groups makes advocacy easier, more enjoyable, and often more effective. Consequently, most of this material was developed for use by groups. Many of its suggestions assume the formation of a group, and joint activities with other groups.

Either way, the ideas presented are intended to get your imaginations working. Expect to adapt them to your issue or group. And do not think you cannot accomplish anything if you do not belong to an advocacy group.

The starting place in your community may be:

- A faith community or adult Sunday School class;

- A committee within a civic organization or nonprofit board;

- A group of neighbors concerned about a problem (toxic wastes nearby, a crumbling school, an unmarked crossing, a local agency needing volunteers); or

- A group already formed for another purpose (a Rotary Club, Head Start parents, or Junior League).

Members of the group may be diverse, but all should agree there is a problem, share a common interest in seeking solutions to the problem(s), and a willingness to take action. Unless more people assume responsibility for the problems facing American communities, they will get worse. If we work together, they can get better.

But whether as individuals or in groups, this manual has two key audiences. First, it is for advocacy novices: people unskilled in policy advocacy. And, it is for advocacy leaders: experienced advocates in search of good ideas for engaging others. So, each part begins with a story of a successful advocacy effort, or a technique, which you can use in your efforts. There is also a brief Civics Review with information to help guide others through the process. (Those with experience may just skim – or skip - the Civics Review; everybody should draw on their own experience throughout.)

In the Appendix you will find some materials ready to copy - for use as handouts at meetings or workshops on advocacy - along with helpful web sites and recommendations for other resources.

It is not necessary that your group be large or experienced. But once the decision has been made to get involved, the initial steps are clear.

**1** The First Task is to assemble a core group (5-10 is a good size) interested in pursuing the basic training needed to move from knowing little and doing less, to knowing more and accomplishing much.

**2** The Second Task is to find and appoint one or more people to assume initial leadership. It helps if that individual lives in the community, is committed to the effort, and already part of your group.

**3** The Third Task is to find a home for the activity. That means meeting space, a telephone, and an e-mail account (e.g., you might get borrowed space in a local nonprofit, at a faith community facility, or community center; the telephone and computer connections can be as low-cost as a loaned cell phone and free net e-mail account at a cyber cafe). Support and encouragement would be a bonus.

It could start out as a project of an existing organization, as an entirely new entity, or as a project of something else but with a timetable for future independence. Whatever the arrangement, moral support will be very important.

**And now, it is time to begin.**

# A Quiz

**Can you imagine yourself doing any of the following?**

---

Calling City Hall to complain about a tax bill you think is too high?  ❏ YES  ❏ NO

---

Helping when your elderly neighbor gets a confusing letter about his Social Security, by making phone calls and dealing with the bureaucracy?  ❏ YES  ❏ NO

---

Making a presentation at your faith group about a community project you care about and know well?  ❏ YES  ❏ NO

---

Responding when your child's school says they may change the rules about whether pregnant teens can stay in school and they want to hear from the parents?  ❏ YES  ❏ NO

---

Testifying before a state legislative committee as part of a panel, about a bill affecting something you know well and care about?  ❏ YES  ❏ NO

PART

01

# Thinking About Democracy

If you answered, "yes" to any of the quiz questions, then you are an advocate, because each is an example of advocacy.

- The first is "self-advocacy," something we do all the time when we speak up for ourselves or our families.

- The second is an example of "case advocacy," which often involves helping someone deal with a complicated bureaucracy.

- The third is an example of "public (or community) education," which is another form of advocacy.

- The fourth is an example of "administrative (or regulatory) advocacy," which includes responding in writing when a governmental unit proposes a change in its rules and invites public comment.

- And fifth is an example of "legislative advocacy." Almost anything done to influence a legislator's vote – testifying, speaking, writing a letter...

Many people hesitate to get involved in advocacy because they equate it with activities they are not comfortable with – like demonstrations at the Capitol or public protest. Those are legitimate advocacy strategies, but they are only part of the story.

"Advocacy" covers a range of activities broad enough to include just about everyone, in just about any kind of setting. And most are things we already do for our neighbors, our friends, and ourselves. Policy advocacy just carries that activity into the policy arena.

> "Many people hesitate to get involved in advocacy because they equate it with activities they are not comfortable with."

**It helps to keep a few underlying principles in mind.**

- Advocacy assumes that people have rights, and those rights are enforceable;

- Advocacy works best when focused on something specific;

- Advocacy is chiefly concerned with rights or benefits to which someone is already entitled; and

- And policy advocacy in particular is concerned with ensuring that institutions work the way they should.

These last two points are related. You have a right to accurate tax bills; your neighbor has a right to his Social Security. Speaking up to protect such rights is not unreasonable.

You would not just pay unfair tax bills or give your neighbor a list of soup kitchens and suggest he adjust to life without Social Security. Instead, you take action to make certain that the government systems involved (the tax office, the Social Security agency) operate according to the law. That is part of policy advocacy.

---

**Anyone can be a policy advocate who is willing to:**

- Speak up;

- Help others get services or benefits to which they are entitled;

- Challenge government systems when they do not work;

- Work for, and vote for, laws, budgets, and policies that do work; and

- Be a voice for others (especially those with troubled lives) with policy-makers.

---

Our government is a system that works well for anyone with knowledge of, and access to, the political process. It works less well for those who either do not know how to get involved, or who face problems in getting involved – like children, low-income families, and those with mental or physical disabilities.

# Six Good Reasons to Get Involved

This is where you come in. As Americans we pride ourselves on having a system that is fair and open to all no matter what their age, or income, or race. But that does not just happen by accident, and neither will prior years' victories stay won without vigilance.

Left on their own, some groups (e.g., foster children, victims of domestic violence or environmental destruction, people with Alzheimer's) tend to be voiceless. How they fare in the political process depends on the role that others are willing to play on their behalf. And when those others (i.e., you and me) fail to get involved, too often the voiceless get left out.

Fortunately, when more of us get involved, wonderful things can happen. All of the legislative victories of recent decades – civil rights for people with disabilities, electoral reforms, environmental protections, child care for working parents, cleaner air and water, nursing home reforms, food safety, and many, many more – are the direct result of advocacy. They represent a tremendous achievement through which millions of Americans have been helped to a better life, and in which millions of ordinary Americans can take pride.

Getting involved will not always yield victory, but not getting involved never does.

Besides, advocacy is fun. There is a tremendous exhilaration in winning, as well as a lot of satisfaction just in trying. But if making your corner of the world a better place and having a good time are not reason enough, here are six more.

## 1. CHARITY IS NOT ENOUGH

A lot can be accomplished by caring people who offer a helping hand. It is great to volunteer at a shelter, or donate toys to the local hospital.  But that will not always be enough.

Donated toys are no substitute for a way to pay the rent, and families with a disabled family member do not need a shelter nearby so much as they need affordable housing and access to home-based care. Volunteers cannot answer either of those needs unless they are also working for public policies to ensure the availability of low-cost housing or of the home-based services so many families need.

> "Without better public policies, many people will lack what they need to be productive members of their communities."

The Reverend William Sloan Coffin, long-time chaplain at Yale University, put it succinctly: "Charity," he wrote, "is a matter of personal attribute, justice a matter of public policy. Never can the first be a substitute for the second."

That is where policy advocacy comes in. Without better public policies, many people will lack what they need to be productive members of their communities.

## 2. ADVOCACY HAS A ROLE FOR EVERYONE

It is possible to be an advocate by informing others, writing or calling a policy-maker, organizing a grassroots campaign, or helping in the background – e.g., doing some research or writing a check.

Advocates for better social policies can be found anywhere: in public agencies and private; in clinical settings and direct service projects; among volunteers and professionals; on the boards of community agencies and business roundtables; whether voted into office or just plain voting.

Sometimes individual effort is all that is needed. A Texas social worker with an irregular work schedule used to monitor the weekly City Council meetings whenever possible. One day she heard a dog owner complain to the City Council about the unfairness of making him pay a license fee while cat owners paid none (a differential the Council chose to ignore).

Some time later she heard the Council consider a proposal to cut services at a mental health clinic, for lack of what seemed a relatively modest sum. During a break she called the pound and the SPCA, collecting estimates of the number of cats in the area. Then she made a quick calculation, which she passed to one of the Council members. It showed that if the same fee required of dogs were also applied to all of the cats, there would be enough money to avoid a cut in mental health services – and dogs would win equity with cats. The Council agreed, and the services were saved.

## 3. SOME PROBLEMS REQUIRE A BROAD ATTACK

Some issues are too big and far too complex to be easily resolved with a few phone calls and a back-of-envelope calculation. Medical research is one such case.

Diseases like Parkinson's, Alzheimer's, Leukemia, or ALS, strike their human victims irrespective of income or family background. And everyone who has ever been diagnosed with a life-threatening or degenerative disease has needed help along the way – some of it provided by family members and volunteers.

But they also need hope: that such terrible diseases can be stopped, or at least slowed down. For that they need more than the help of a kindly volunteer or dedicated family member, more than the assistance available from local faith-based groups and community programs – they need sophisticated medical care and expensive, ground-breaking research. That is why there is advocacy to persuade Congress and the White House to allow the use of federal funds for stem cell and other basic research, and why such efforts routinely attract such broad, bi-partisan support.

Slowing the rate of environmental destruction offers another case in point. Small efforts are important, and individuals can play a critical role, but at some point governments, public policies, and broad citizen consensus are also required.

In 1970 environmental consciousness was chiefly the province of small, hardy bands of committed groups and their largely volunteer memberships. Most Americans did not have a clear idea that they could – or should – be involved. Then one U.S. Senator, Gaylord Nelson of Wisconsin, called for a nationwide "teach in" on the environment. Working out of borrowed space, with a skeleton staff and energetic students everywhere, the first-ever Earth Day was held on April 22, 1970. That first year an estimated 20 million people and thousands of schools participated. Congress shut down for the day, as 500 members of Congress spread out across the country to take part.

Now it is an annual event. By Earth Day 2001, it was estimated that over 200 million people were participating, in 140 countries worldwide. Public attitudes everywhere had undergone a sea change. And perhaps most significant, in the time since the first Earth Day, the U.S. Congress had adopted a Clean Air Act, a Clean Water Act, an Endangered Species Act, and created an Environmental Protection Agency. On the international front change was also visible, as multi-national agreements were being struck on global warming, energy efficiency, and the ways in which human rights and the environment are linked.

It is true that efforts on this scale require a high level of sophistication: knowledge of the laws, the efforts of organized groups, the help of professional lobbyists, and sustained activity over a period of months or even years. Some of those involved have been pressing their case for decades.

But it is also true that each step along the way meant the involvement of countless ordinary people along with the professionals, and each victory also meant a better quality of life for many – including those in poor communities and rural areas where resources are scarce.

Any time we insist on helping only through one-on-one, voluntary activity, we make others dependent on the whims and fashions of charity. And we effectively write off everyone who lives where the charity (or volunteer) that is needed is not available, or whose conditions stem from something too big for one person, one volunteer to address.

> "Any time we insist on helping only through one-on-one, voluntary activity, we make others dependent on the whims and fashions of charity."

## 4. GOVERNMENT POLICIES AFFECT EVERYONE

There are also self-interested reasons to get involved, whether the people needing advocacy are related to us or not. Everyone with an interest in the future, for example, has a personal stake in policies for children, as does everyone who hopes to get old. Marian Wright Edelman, President of the Children's Defense Fund, once remarked that, depending on what we do now for the children, before long they will be either... supporting us, depending on us, or shooting at us. In the same way we all have a stake in what happens to the air we breathe, the wages we earn, the products we buy, and the quality of life in our communities.

**Every level of government is important and plays a part. Some examples:**

- Local school boards are responsible for the schools;
- County and city governments operate hospitals, make grants for the arts, and protect the local environment;
- State governments decide whether everything from nursing homes to child care is licensed and affordable; and
- Federal laws affect every aspect of our lives—agriculture, education, elder care, environmental policy—and much, much more…

Visionary members of the business community understand. They reach out to meet immediate needs, e.g., by mentoring or forming partnerships with individual schools, but they also work through the political process to improve conditions in all the schools. Business leaders in Chicago, for example, lobbied their state legislature on behalf of education reforms. Similarly, on the national scene, the business executives who make up the Committee for Economic Development have been powerful advocates for greater government investments in prenatal care, childcare, education, and the arts.

## 5. DEMOCRACY IS NOT A SPECTATOR SPORT

In a democracy where every voice and vote count, doing nothing is a political act; it is a vote for the status quo. Staying out of the process does not mean that laws will not get passed; it just means they will get passed without reflecting your priorities and wishes, or those of anyone you might speak for – especially those who have been disabled or abused, ill or in pain, troubled or poor.

If you feel intimidated or uncomfortable at the thought of speaking up or otherwise getting involved... if you have been thinking it is enough to be informed about the issues and cast your vote intelligently... then it is time to think again.

If you went to a restaurant just to read the menu you would be informed – but you would be missing the point. Ultimately you have to decide what you want, what you are willing to pay for it, and be willing to engage with other people to get it.

That also applies to your role as a citizen in a democracy: being informed is not enough. You have to decide what you want from your government, what you are willing to pay for it, and engage with your elected representatives so they can help you get it.

## 6. POLITICIANS ARE PEOPLE TOO

Many city, county, and state elected officials work part-time in their political roles (often for very little pay), and the rest of the time in their family/bread-winning roles. They have little or no paid staff, and no magic way of knowing what is on the voters' minds. Nor can they afford fancy polls, focus groups, or surveys. "Feeling the pulse," as a local official in Indiana said, "is often accidental." Unless constituents tell them, they do not know what people think.

"Another problem arises when legislators must vote on matters outside their personal experience, and do not have any real feeling for the consequences of their votes."

Another problem arises when legislators must vote on matters outside their personal experience, and do not have any real feeling for the consequences of their votes. That is why a Utah state Senator tells advocates to expose their elected officials to their issues in very human, personal ways. Invite them to spend an hour or two with emotionally troubled children, she suggests, or to have dinner at the home of a family in subsidized housing. This is a challenge just ripe for creative solutions.

A national program called "Walk A Mile In Your Sister's Shoes" used this approach. Working with state and local groups, they pair low-income women on assistance with a local, state, or federal elected official for a month, and ask them to participate in at least one shared activity each week. In addition, the elected officials are asked to put their families on a food budget comparable to what low-income families get from food stamps. State legislators have found themselves stranded when their sister's old beater car breaks down (and there is no money for AAA or towing) or spending long hours waiting for their sister to be re-certified for Medicaid or food stamps. Without direct experience, it is hard for middle class legislators to appreciate the practical affect of the decisions they make (e.g., requiring frequent re-certifications, limiting the value of the cars owned by working people who use food stamps or Medicaid to supplement low wages).

A St. Louis group called ROWEL (for the sharp-pronged wheel on a stirrup that prods a horse – or Missouri mule – into action) designed a simulation that uses 15-minute time blocks to correspond to a week in the life of a low-income family. Elected officials and community members play the part of someone who is elderly, disabled, or just needing help (short- or long-term), while others play the parts of such community resources as a food bank, pawnshop, grocery store, the food stamp and social service agencies, the police, a landlord. During the Simulation participants are subject to all the rules governing assistance in their community and told that their job is to survive one month. The experience, however brief, reveals how hard it is to be poor in America – and how difficult it can be to get help. One local Judge who participated said he finally understood the frustration low-income people express at "the system".

Above all, advocacy is a frame of mind. As everything mentioned thus far should make clear, advocacy is first and foremost a mindset – often not a job title, occupation, or role in life. Whether it involves a single individual like the woman in Texas or a group with staff like Walk A Mile, advocates see opportunities when others only see obstacles, and work to change the institutions that cause problems for everyone, rather than wait until after the damage is done or be satisfied with easing problems one-by-one.

## Take Five...

Just like the famous Paul Desmond refrain, here is something deceptively simple – and as likely to stay with you.

Experienced advocates know three things.

1. **Phone and letter campaigns remain effective.** Elected officials (and their staff) note the issues that generate the most letters and calls; they are a useful gauge of community support for/against an issue. And

2. **Broad appeals for action do not work.** Alerts that sound too general, or too complicated, get set aside.

3. **The competition for attention is keen.** By now, there are so many groups sending out e-mails and snail mails requesting action that readers ignore much of what comes their way. And groups with tight budgets cannot afford to waste scarce resources and/or staff time for long alerts that do not get results.

But if you want your appeals to produce results: make taking action easy; make it time-limited; and design it to fit into busy lives. Here is one version that gets results.

A few years ago Univeristy of Washington social work students tried to get other students to write letters about legislative proposals they thought might harm children, but the answers they got just seemed like excuses. In response to their pleas, people said:

- **I don't have time**
- **I don't know what to say**
- **I don't know my legislator**
- **I don't know the address**
- **I don't have any envelopes/paper/stamps**
- **I can't**

To their credit, the students took the excuses seriously, treating them as real barriers to be eliminated. In the process they developed *"Take Five For Kids"* – a way to be an advocate for children in just five minutes or less.

At a strategically located table, during lunch hour, they provided answers to all the excuses: sample letters, brief fact sheets, people to answer questions, blank paper/envelopes/cell-phones/laptops, plus the names and addresses of all the legislators. Visible to all was a big sign reading: *Take Five For Kids*.

Right off the bat, they generated a couple dozen letters. A week later they were back at their table with new information – and this time they got twice as many letters. Before long, people were referring to the *"Take Five Tables"* and inventing variations.

Some advocates have adapted the idea by renaming and re-formatting their legislative alerts, with a section for "actions you can take in 5 minutes or less," or, *"Take Five For… (housing, or whales, or…)."* Like the students at their table, these alerts include all the key ingredients, in a simple, easy-to-accomplish format that enables concerned citizens to fit advocacy into busy lives.

On a single page handout, usually within a text box, give brief information, brief messages, and all the information needed to contact a legislator by mail, e-mail, or phone. Clip art can supply a clock.

> **"With only two days at the tables, we got 271 letters signed in support of the bill!"**

People who get *Take Five* alerts in written form say they prop them on their telephones or computer keyboards every week until they have made their calls or written letters. (Guilt, they admit, is part of what makes it work: "you mean I couldn't take 5 minutes a week to help out?") Those who work for public agencies get their *Take Five* alerts at home. They cannot lobby while on the public payroll, but on their own time they are citizens like anybody else, and lobbying is allowed.

*Take Five* tables are popping up everywhere: in the lobbies of social agencies and children's hospitals, after services on Sunday, at PTA meetings or professional meetings. One group set up a *Take Five* table at the beginning of the cross-Iowa bike ride, hoping to expand their network in support of a new bicycle helmet law. They got 400 members signed up in just a couple of hours. Women eager to see the Violence Against Women Act renewed in 2000 set up *Take Five* tables beside the Silent Witness silhouettes of women murdered in domestic violence: over 400 letters resulted. Psychology students at the University of Utah set up tables in the cafeteria, seeking letters in support of higher education for foster children; they got over seven hundred during the course of a week.

As one participant reported later, "With only two days (four hours each) at the tables, we got 271 letters signed in support of the bill! I am so thrilled at this success not only for the bill, but for the amazing number of students that wanted to get involved and learn a little more about the legislative process (not to mention learning who their legislator was!)"

*Take Five* alerts and tables work to: generate letters, sign up members for a grassroots network, and win involvement in a community education campaign. People on the receiving end say that just knowing they can be advocates for something they care about, in five minutes or less, is empowering.

Tips: Because they get so much computer-generated mail, many legislative offices make a distinction between "astro turf messages" (i.e., identical cards or letters that might all be signed by the same person using different pens) and "real grassroots messages." Both are noticed, but real grassroots communications get more attention.

To make sure the letters generated by your *Take Five* tables fall in the "real" category, even when the heart of the letter is identical, have senders do three things:

- Sign and print their names on paper; spell out full name on e-mails.
- Include their home address
- Add a personal note – even something as brief as "I really care" or, "This means a lot to me," sends a message to the staff opening the mail.

**The possibilities are endless….**

# The Three-Legged Stool

In 1995 a group of child advocates in Washington State began conducting an annual 3-day Advocacy Camp, a place to train advocacy leaders for more effective work statewide. The framework developed for Advocacy Camp offers a good way to think about, and plan for, advocacy work. The basic idea is simple: Good Advocacy rests on a Three-legged Stool; to be effective, all three legs must be in place.

### ONE: THE CAPITOL LEG

> "Good Advocacy rests on a Three-legged Stool; to be effective, all three legs must be in place."

This leg of the stool refers to everything that goes on where the laws and policies are made: city or county council, state legislature, U.S. Congress. That is where you have full or part-time lobbyists, where you hold lobby days or go to testify, where someone sends out regular alerts, where citizens go to meet with their legislators during the Legislative Session, where you can meet with people who staff the Legislators and the various Committees. And, after an ordinance or law is passed, this is where you meet with staff from Executive Branch agencies to work out plans for implementation of the laws.

### TWO: THE COMMUNITY, OR GRASSROOTS, LEG

This leg of the stool refers to everything that goes on in the community. This is where you set up your telephone trees and e-mail lists for responding to the alerts coming out of the Capitol; it is where you set up "Take 5 Tables" to generate cards and letters or sign people up for your networks. It is the place where grassroots campaigns take root; it is where you do community education, sponsor community/candidate forums, and host "site visits" by your elected officials.

### THREE: THE MEDIA LEG

This leg of the stool refers to everything we do to spread the word to more people, whether through establishment media – local radio, TV, & newspapers – or through informal media like professional newsletters, congregation bulletins, apartment house notice boards, Facebook and Twitter. We need this leg for three reasons – first because elected officials pay attention to the media; second because we need to reach more people than those already informed and persuaded, and third because we have to deliberately counter the inaccurate, misinformation that shows up all too often in the popular media.

**Here are three helpful points to keep in mind:**

*1. Two of the three legs are firmly planted where you live.*
   The work done in the Legislative or Congressional District is as important as the work being done in the Capitol.

## 2. *You need not cover all three legs of the stool alone.*

You can work with other groups to see that all three are getting attention. For example, on an issue like childcare (which affects people of all incomes, and children of all ages, children with disabilities and children whose parents work the night shift), it is easy to think of ways to share the workload:

- To cover the Capitol Leg: think of groups already lobbying in the Capitol – early childhood education professionals, statewide child advocacy groups, women's organizations, faith communities (which is where a lot of child care is located).

- To handle the Media Leg: think of approaching a local community college or university communications program, or a local Junior League group.

- To take the lead on the Community Leg: think of asking the PTA, a women's group, Kids Count leaders, or perhaps a supportive business group.

## 3. *Do not worry if you do not have all three legs in place from the start.*

Work with your strengths, and build from experience. Just aim to have the three legs in place within a reasonable time frame, like one to two years.

---

### Subways Are For Speaking Up

In the stories and examples that follow, look for evidence of the three-legged stool. I picked up one of my favorite, least-costly advocacy techniques one morning on the subway in Washington, D.C. The car was packed with tourists, though I noticed a woman I know about two-thirds of the way down the car. We waved to each other and smiled. Then, just as the subway lurched into motion she called my name: "Hey Nancy." When I turned to look at her she asked, "Did you see what the Senate Finance Committee did yesterday?" I felt so mortified; right out there in public she was striking up a conversation about something I could read in my newspaper. But I had acknowledged her, so I could not pretend I had not heard.

"No," I called back, "what happened?" "Well," she said, "they did something yesterday that is going to affect every working family in America! And I will bet most people do not even know about it yet." At that, heads all over the subway car perked up, and just as suddenly, I caught on.

From then until we reached the next subway stop, I fed her straight lines ("oh no… that is terrible… tell me more…."), and she spelled out more details. Soon those tourists were like people at a ping-pong match, heads swiveling back and forth to follow our conversation.

When she got off, I rushed to catch up with her in the station. "What you just did was wonderful," I said, "those people were just 'lobbied' by a pro. Do you do that very often?" "Oh sure," she replied, "I do it all the time. I'm especially fond of elevators – you know, they cannot get off."

PART
02

# A Civics Review

In just a few minutes that woman on the subway had reminded me what good advocacy is all about: speaking up, and seizing opportunities – in this case with one of the most powerful groups of all, the voters.

Every time I tell this story, listeners make up their own variations: one woman uses trips to the grocery store with her son to educate other shoppers about third-world issues, another now routinely lobbies other voters at her exercise class. And two men report they have turned the corridors of their office building into classes on child abuse policies. Two home care workers who live near their state Capitol say they use any free time between appointments to ride the elevators and discuss their current concerns. Grocery store lines, long waits at stoplights, waiting to get into a movie; for any captive audience the advocacy possibilities are endless.

"Policy advocacy efforts often depend on understanding how federal, state, and local government works."

As my friend on the subway made so clear, you do not have to be an expert to make a difference, and you do not have to go to Washington, DC or your state capitol to lobby. Good advocates make opportunities everywhere they go. But your group's effectiveness (and ability to do more than just raise an issue) will often depend on getting directly involved in the policy process, and for that it is important to be reminded how the process works.

Unless you happen to live in a state capitol or work in a government job, it is easy to forget the things we all learned in social studies class. But policy advocacy efforts often depend on understanding how federal, state, and local government works. By getting involved you are likely to become a better, more knowledgeable citizen and voter.

There are always new faces to learn, and from time to time the details change, but the basics have not changed since whenever you last had to learn them. And the best news is that there are points of influence at every level of government. "All politics is local" – that is, politics at any level has local consequences. And with your elected officials at every level, you have "the butter", the ability to wield some influence. Best of all, the techniques you learn by dealing with local school boards or city council members are the same techniques you will use in dealing with state legislators or U.S. Senators.

## The System

There are three branches of government: a *Legislative* branch, which enacts laws; an *Executive* branch which carries out laws; and a *Judicial* branch, which interprets laws (and resolves any conflicts between the other two branches).

## LEGISLATIVE

*Congress is the federal legislative body;* it consists of the Senate and House of Representatives, has a large staff (about 30,000 people), and meets year-round. Every state has two U.S. Senators and at least one Representative (roughly one Representative for every 650,000 people).

*State legislatures also consists of a Senate and House* (in every state but Nebraska) though the lower house is sometimes called the Assembly; many state legislatures have little or no staff and most meet for a limited number of days each year (nine are in session all year; a few only meet every other year).

*City and County Councils are the most common form of local legislature.* Some states have regional bodies as well (e.g., responsible for transportation or energy).

Anyone living in one of the 50 states is represented by: two U.S. Senators and one U.S. Representative in the *Federal* Congress; one Senator and one or more Representative in their *state* legislature; plus City and County Council members at the *local* level. We get to vote for all of them, and we have the right to indicate how we wish to be represented by all of them.

## EXECUTIVE

The *federal executive branch* consists of the President and Vice President, 15 Cabinet-level departments (for example, the Department of Education), and 70 independent agencies (like the Environmental Protection Agency). Including members of the armed forces, over 4 million civilian and military employees work for the executive branch of the federal government, nationwide.

"Rule-making responsibilities are typically housed in each executive branch agency."

Each *state executive branch* is headed by a Governor and Lieutenant Governor, with various Cabinet-level departments (like a Department of Human Resources); many also have independent agencies, boards, or commissions (e.g., for Higher Education or some time-limited issue).

Each *local executive branch* is typically headed by a Mayor, County Executive, and/or town manager, along with various local agencies (e.g., a County Department of Public Health, a Transit Authority, city police and fire departments) to complete the picture. (Some local bodies, such as school boards and city councils, may also perform legislative functions.)

At every level, executive branch agencies use rule-making or regulatory functions to spell out in Regulations the details by which the laws passed by the legislative branch will be carried out. Rule-making responsibilities are typically housed in each executive branch agency. The regulatory agencies also have powers of enforcement for existing laws and regulations. For example, the Environmental Protection Agency enforces clean air standards and state Public Utility Commissions set rates for utilities.

## JUDICIAL

The *federal Judiciary* consists of the Supreme Court, the U.S. Court of Appeals, and the U.S. District Court. Federal judges are appointed.

States also have trial courts and appellate courts, including the equivalent of a Supreme Court. The names of these courts vary greatly from state to state. State court judges may be appointed or elected.

At the local level there are Municipal Courts, plus Justice of the Peace Courts and Small Claims Courts.

The beauty of our system of government is that ultimately *we*, not some agency or official, *are the government*. And each of the branches, at every level, is susceptible to citizen influence – to a greater or lesser degree.

All three branches of government, at every level, are directly accountable to us, the citizens. We just have to vote to have a voice. In addition we can: use the media to expose problems, serve on advisory groups or as members of good government organizations, sponsor candidate forums, communicate with our elected officials, be good citizens – in short, we just have to be involved.

# Influencing the System

## THE LEGISLATIVE BRANCH

The ways in which citizens can influence legislative branch activity are almost limitless. Some of the many things citizens can do include:

- Suggest ideas for laws and draft them up;

- Build public support and educate others about an issue;

- Draw attention to proposed laws by working with the media;

- Testify as to the merits of bills you care about;

- Analyze budgets and offer alternatives; and

- Lobby for, or against, passage of various bills and budget items.

Some situations offer special opportunities. For example, the fact that most state legislators have little or no paid staff makes them heavily reliant on citizens to offer ideas for legislation, provide the research, and even identify potential witnesses for hearings. In effect citizens can act as "staff" for the legislators (some actually work in their legislators' offices as volunteers). At the national level, where there is paid staff, meeting with staff can often be as good as (or better than) meeting with their bosses. They can always use the help of good advocates.

Advocacy groups have a special role to play. For example, they can bring up issues that would otherwise get missed (like the lack of services for emotionally troubled youth). Advocates can assure that those directly affected (in this case, the families of troubled teens) do not find themselves waging lonely battles for better policies. And advocates can push the limits of a debate, thus insuring that something more than the easy, politically popular causes, gets attention.

Sometimes advocates build on past victories. On the federal level, a series of stunning legislative victories has been won by advocates for people with disabilities (who used all of these techniques – drafting laws, testifying, using media, staging protests, lobbying for passage). In 1975 they won passage of the Education for all Handicapped Children Act. Then, after years of struggle, they convinced the Congress and the President that it is in the national interest to go a step farther. In 1990 they won passage of the ADA – the Americans with Disabilities Act. That law extends the protections of the Civil Rights Act to everyone with physical or mental disabilities by ensuring equal access to employment, state and local government programs, and the benefits of life enjoyed by all Americans.

A few years later they built on the heightened visibility won through the ADA fight to win improvements affecting education, and the EHCA became IDEA – Individuals with Disabilities Education Act. Together they are transforming the lives of millions of Americans with disabilities, and everyone who shares their communities.

Those laws did not come from some Senator, Representative, or well-paid lobbyist; they sprang directly from the mouths, pens, fact sheets, lives, and lobbying of countless people with disabilities, their families, friends, and advocates. When each of those bills was signed by a President, it marked one more victory – won not by some wealthy, insider elite, but by ordinary citizens and those most directly affected.

## THE EXECUTIVE BRANCH

Citizens can influence executive branch policy in many ways. They can:

■ Monitor program operation or serve as volunteers;

■ Serve on agency advisory bodies;

■ File comments on the regulations that govern how programs are implemented;

■ Call public attention to proposed regulations;

■ Ask their elected representatives to monitor programs and comment on draft regulations;

■ Challenge policies or regulations in the courts whenever they prove inconsistent with the law; and

■ Participate in the decision making process of an agency.

Policy advocates play a critical role when they work to influence the regulations that carry out laws. It is an activity that has proved to be increasingly important.

Laws are often written in language that is deliberately vague. So, after a law is passed, the relevant executive branch agency has to draw up regulations – which are the rules that actually govern day-to-day operation of the programs. Thanks to the Administrative Procedure Act (APA), every proposed federal regulation has to be published in a document called the *Federal Register* (which is available in every government depository library, many local public libraries, and on-line at www.nara.gov). Citizens must be given an opportunity to recommend changes in the regulations before they are finalized. (Similar processes and publications exist in most states, though not every state has a law like the APA.) The opportunity to comment can be a formidable power, especially since once they are issued in final form; *regulations have the force of law.*

**"Laws are often written in language that is deliberately vague."**

The Federal Election Commission (FEC) provides a case in point. In 1999, the FEC was considering new regulations that would govern campaign activity on the Internet, including the efforts of nonprofit groups and individual volunteers. They issued a Notice of Inquiry, requesting comments on a wide range of issues. Many nonprofits were concerned that applying federal election law, which was written with traditional broadcast media in mind, would stifle citizen use of the Internet. They sent out alerts explaining the issues, and providing information about how to comment, to groups all over the country. As a result, the FEC received more than 1300 comments on their proposal! This was unheard of in an agency where a dozen comments would be considered a good response. The comments came from all kinds of groups and their members. As a result, the FEC decided to take a hands-off approach to the Internet, and limited regulation of Internet campaigning to a narrow scope of activities.

Citizen groups can also insure that programs operate as they should on an on-going basis by serving on advisory groups, monitoring programs, and issuing public reports. The day-to-day quality of nursing homes, training programs, public art, or school meals in many communities is directly related to the presence (or absence) of citizens who monitor their operation and publicize the findings. Even something as wide-ranging as the "Stop Sprawl" movement is made up of ordinary citizens, people willing to pay attention to the details of zoning proceedings.

## THE JUDICIARY

The judiciary is less open to citizen influence, but even it offers opportunities. Citizens can:

- Participate in Friend-of-the-Court (Amicus) briefs;
- File, threaten, or cooperate in a lawsuit;
- Take part in an appeals process; or
- Serve as a Court Appointed Special Advocate (CASA), Guardian Ad Litem – or similar program associated with the courts.

The Judiciary is rightly thought of as the branch of government least susceptible to citizen influence, but that is true chiefly in terms of traditional lobbying. We cannot (and should not) try to lobby judges. But that is not the only way for citizens to have an impact through the courts. Lawsuits, complaints, and Friend-of-the-Court briefs are all useful tools.

A *lawsuit* forced the Social Security Administration to include autism, mental impairments, and other severe disabilities in children as grounds for Supplemental Security Income eligibility. Because advocates spoke up and refused to be brushed aside (the effort took seven years), over half-a-million children from families with modest incomes now get help.

At the local level, sometimes the *threat of a lawsuit* is enough to get action – for example, from a school district that is dragging its feet under IDEA – the Individuals with Disabilities Education Act – and refusing to mainstream children with disabilities.

Or, citizens can file *complaints* if they believe a law is being ignored. Citizen complaints have resulted in better action on child/adult abuse reports, more thorough investigations by nursing home licensing bodies, and increased access to public transportation for people with physical limitations. This has worked for environmental groups if they find agencies delaying implementation of regulations or misconstruing the intent of the law.

Sometimes the best vehicle for judicial participation is by filing, or agreeing to sign onto, a *Friend-of-the-Court brief* which lays out the views of people with direct knowledge of the impact a Court decision is likely to have. E.g., Courts at all levels want to get a broad spectrum of public opinion on the right-to-die issue from religious, consumer, and advocacy organizations – particularly as more cases involving the terminally ill and people in "a persistent vegetative state," move through the courts.

And advocates can help others go through an *administrative appeals process* whenever they feel a benefit has been unfairly denied by the wording or application of the relevant regulations. Appeals of benefit denials are won far more often when a claimant is accompanied by knowledgeable advocate. And while it is often possible to get help from a legal services or legal aid office, the advocate in an appeal need not be a lawyer or even a paralegal – knowledgeable advocates come from many backgrounds.

## DO NOT FORGET LOCAL GOVERNMENT

Perhaps the most overlooked target for influence is local government. Citizens who remember to write or call their state or federal representatives often forget to use the influence they have in their *local* communities – even though it probably is greatest there. Consider all of the ways in which schools, hospitals, the arts, and social agencies get public support: e.g., through tax breaks, gifts, in-kind support, tax-exempt donations, and special zoning provisions. You can use that support as leverage whenever a tax-supported institution fails to meet the needs of citizens. And the results can be dramatic.

Anti-hunger advocates in Pittsburgh persuaded their city government to create a food policy commission. The Commission took up such issues as how to keep grocery stores in low-income neighborhoods, and whether public transportation routes are convenient to the grocery stores. Creating the Commission required educating both the public and elected officials alike, and took time, but the results were worth it.

One clear advantage of working locally is that frequently the advocacy issues may spring up, and get settled, fast. After the Monroe (Indiana) County Council voted 4-3 to cut funding for the Stonebelt Center for the Disabled (a facility for people with developmental disabilities), a phone call alerting friends of the Center helped turn the issue around. Once alerted, family, friends, clients, and professionals familiar with the Center's work decided to ask that the vote be reconsidered. It took only 40-50 people at the next Council meeting a few weeks later, but many of them – clients included – spoke up. Council members were so impressed that by the end of the evening they voted unanimously to rescind the earlier cuts.

A consumer group in Florida was equally effective. When they learned that a nearby hospital wanted to build a new clinic, they pressured their local health agency to hold public hearings on the hospital's request – and then provided evidence that the hospital had been turning away low-income patients. Thanks to the public hearing, attention was focused on the problem, the hospital agreed to change its policies, and the clinic got built.

## BASIC TOOLS

There are three basic ways to communicate your views: you can *write*, you can *call*, or you can *visit*. And there are always three audiences for your letters, calls and visits. The first is *policy makers and their staff*; the second audience is *other voters*; and the third is the *media*. As noted in Part I, to have a three-legged stool firmly in place, all three are important.

### 1. Writing a Legislator or Policy Maker

Politicians and other decision-makers pay attention to their mail. Most offices keep a running tally of the e-mail coming in; it helps them know what their constituents care about. Responding to concerned citizens is good politics and crucial to survival. Every letter counts, but a personal letter is always more effective than a form letter or petition. After the terrorist attacks on September 11, 2001, many Senators and Representatives began advising constituents to use e-mail or regular mail for the district offices back in the home state, but only e-mail or fax for communication with their offices in Washington, DC. A quick phone call or e-mail will let you know what method your Senators and Representative prefer.

> "Most state legislators say 10-15 letters on a single issue will get their attention."

Most state legislators say *10-15 letters* on a single issue will get their attention. To a part-time legislator with little or no paid staff, three or four dozen letters loom very large. The same is true for agency officials, county commissioners, and city council members.

E-mail is a bit of a special case. In 2000, Congress received 80 million e-mail messages. That number has since doubled, with more than 200 million e-mails going to Congress every year. On an average day during the 107th Congress, the House received over 230,000 messages, and the Senate received over 88,009 messages. Volume on that scale is difficult to manage – let alone respond to. State and local officials may have even less ability to deal with e-mail. That is one reason many have turned to web services to get some control over e-mail – screening out spam and junk mail, and limiting easy access to people from the home state.

Two practical pieces of advice should be followed. First, keep in mind that elected officials are like any other group: some are comfortable with e-mail, others are not. So, ask whether the people you wish to contact like getting e-mail – if they say "no," do not use it. Second, if they say "yes," always include your real name and home address. Catchy e-mail monikers (like "fun gal" or "tough guy") may be cute, but they do not convey whether you are a constituent. Since elected officials always try to respond to constituents, your home address is essential.

Also keep in mind that legislators who use laptops can get e-mail messages with no intermediary. Regular mail goes to an aide to be opened (and sometimes summarized); e-mails may go directly to the legislator.

### Letters/e-mails to policy makers (all levels) should:

- Be concise, informed, and polite (do not threaten, do not be rude);

- Be brief (1-2 pages, a few paragraphs) and legible;

- State your purpose in the first paragraph; and

- Include your full name and home address.

### If your letter is about a bill, budget item, or specific policy:

- Cite the bill, policy, or budget item (by name or number if you know it, or just stated clearly if you do not); if you plan to mention two issues/bills – state that up front;

- Say whether you support or oppose it, and briefly why;

- Be factual and speak from your own experience or knowledge; and

- Ask for their views on the issue or bill.

Your letters do not need to be on fancy stationery or written in technical, legal language. At a time when mass-produced letters are common, handwritten notes are often the most powerful. A rough letter, any letter, is always better than no letter at all.

## 2. Calling a Legislator or Policy Maker

Politicians and decision-makers also pay attention when citizens take the trouble to call and convey their views, and the same general rules apply. Let them know concisely: who you are, what you are calling about, and what you want from them (e.g., support for a bill, opposition to a budget cut, action on a proposal). If there is a message machine, state who you are, what you want them to support or reject, and then spell out your name and address. Delaware Governor Ruth Ann Minner reflects a view represented in surveys, namely that elected officials like phone conversations because they provide instant feedback. And, she adds, always follow a phone call with a note. That way, if the elected official did not have a pen and paper handy, they will have a record of your call – and either way you get a second chance to make your point.

Some states have toll-free lines into their Capitol while the legislature is in session. Operators help callers identify their Senator and Representative, as well as bill numbers. With a single toll-free call – usually requiring just a couple of minutes – messages can be sent to Senator, Representative, and/or Governor. (If your state does not have a toll-free line to the Capitol, advocating for one and involving high school students in the effort, would be a great project.)

A California group made a short video showing calls made to leave a message at their Governor's office. Viewers could hear the polite staff taking it down, while the number flashed at the bottom of the screen.

The U.S. Capitol has a switchboard number – (202) 224-3121 – that is answered 24 hours a day, 7 days a week. Operators will transfer you to your Senator or Representative's office. You can reach staff during the day, but after hours, you can leave a message.

**Note:** Calls are an especially good task for the politically shy because as often as not, calls are answered by a receptionist, operator, or machine. Callers just need to leave a brief message, name, address, and/or phone number. No questions are asked, no positions are challenged.

### 3. Visiting a Legislator or Policy Maker

"It helps to have ready a short, 60-second version of what you want to say."

Elected officials can be visited on the job (in Washington, D.C., the State Capitol, in City or County Council chambers), in their local offices, or whenever they are engaged in public business (e.g., at a rally or parade, at a fundraiser or speech appearance, in the statehouse corridors, or at a town hall meeting). When the legislature is in session, about the only occasions that are off limits are those which are obviously personal or family occasions. The wife of one former Governor still speaks with feeling about the people who would approach her husband at family funerals and other personal events; that is NOT an effective way to lobby.

Often you will only get a few minutes to make your point so it helps to have ready a short, 60-second version of what you want to say (something you can say in the time it takes to shake hands or walk someone to the elevator). And it is always smart to use that 60-second version first thing; if there is time, follow that with more details – like the impact in the legislator's district, or a more elaborate version of your message.

## A visit to a policy maker (all kinds) should always include five things:

| | | |
|---|---|---|
| **1** | **Who you are and where you live (so they know you have the butter).** | I'm Kim Q Citizen, and I live in your district... |
| **2** | **Any group you belong to which is working on the issue, and the number involved (more butter).** | I belong to the 350-member Association of Pizza Lovers... |
| **3** | **What you came to talk about – in just a phrase or a few words.** | I came to talk about House Bill 1234 – to require public programs to serve pizza three times a week. This bill is supported by a broad coalition of pizza makers, tomato growers, sausage producers, and the local Weight Watchers.... |
| **4** | **What you want them to do (please VOTE FOR... please OPPOSE...).** | We would like you to vote YES when the bill comes before your Committee.... |
| **5** | **Something in writing – a fact sheet or brief explanation of how the issue is important to their legislative or congressional district – with your name, address, phone number and e-mail address.** | Just in case we get interrupted, let me give you this brief Fact Sheet. It has basic information, and tells how you can contact us if you have any questions or would like our help. |

If there is more time, paint a brief word picture of the people who will be affected by their decision, and tell them how you mean to share the results of this meeting with others (e.g., by reporting on it in your congregation newsletter, at a PTA or other meeting). Whenever possible, schedule an appointment in advance, and always thank them for their time or any recent actions of which you approve.

## HOWEVER YOU GO ABOUT IT, IT HELPS TO REMEMBER TWO THINGS:

Just ask! Policy makers will not think you rude for stating what you want, and may think it odd if you do not. Part of their job is to be asked, and part of our job is to ask. In a representative democracy like ours, we have to tell our elected representatives how we wish to be represented.

You cannot be persuasive if you are not understood. If there is any doubt of being understood, avoid jargon, technical terms, or initials (e.g., SCAN means Student Counseling and Assistance Network to some, but to others it is a Scandinavian furniture store); be prepared to go over the basics if necessary.

# Special Tips for the Legislative Process

Very few of the bills introduced in any body become law. In the U.S. Congress as well as most states, only about 10-20% of the bills introduced become law. A classic study by Ron Dear and Rino Patti of the bills introduced over several years in the Washington state legislature yielded seven tactics that were likely to improve a bill's chances of success. The bills that made it out of committee and onto the floor tended to share the following characteristics:

**EARLY INTRODUCTION.** If your state allows bills to be pre-filed before the session formally begins, that is a good time to get your bill introduced. It means there will be more time for legislators to consider it, hold hearings on it, build support for it, raise and answer questions about it.

**MULTIPLE SPONSORS.** A bill that has several sponsors from the outset tends to look more like a winner. Bills with only one sponsor, by contrast, are sometimes assumed to be introduced just to please a constituent or do somebody a favor - but not as a serious legislative proposal.  Multiple sponsors increase credibility, and also the number of advocates working for its success.

**BI-PARTISAN SPONSORSHIP.** It is always essential to have sponsors from the party in the majority, but unless one party overwhelmingly dominates the legislature, it helps a bill's credibility and chances if its sponsors come from both parties. (On the national level, and anywhere that margins are close or party discipline is unreliable, bi-partisan sponsorship is essential.)

> "Since the executive branch will have to administer the resulting program or enforce a law, their support or opposition often influences legislators."

**INFLUENTIAL SPONSORS.** The job of getting a bill through hearings and out to the floor will be much easier if the Chair or highest ranking minority members of the subcommittees and committees are sponsors of the bill. If they, or highly respected senior members of the body, become sponsors and use their influence on its behalf, that is half the battle.

**SUPPORT OF GOVERNOR AND RELEVANT EXECUTIVE AGENCY.** Since the executive branch will have to administer the resulting program or enforce a law, their support or opposition often influences legislators. (In any case the executive branch tends to have data, information, expertise, and enforcement authority). If support is out of the question, the next best option is executive branch neutrality. The worst posture is outright opposition.

**OPEN HEARINGS.** Hearings are a good opportunity to make a public record, bring an issue before the public, get questions and points of opposition out in the open and dealt with, and to give the advocacy groups a rallying point. It is best to get a hearing well before the date of a vote so there is more time for changes to be made and the outcome is less fixed. (Citizens can urge committee members and staff to schedule a meeting.)

**AMENDMENTS.** Some advocates think their proposal has to be enacted exactly as they conceived it. That rarely happens. In fact, bills that are not amended tend to die. That is because everyone who amends a proposal has to be familiar with it and develops a bit of ownership, a stake in its future. (There are exceptions, e.g., "killer amendments" specifically designed to kill a bill.) Be ready to quickly assess an amendment and decide if you support or oppose it. Encourage amendments; often they will increase your bill's chances of success.

Ultimately, even these seven tactics are no guarantee of success. Bills are more likely to pass if they involve low costs, non-controversial beneficiaries and purposes, and little significant change. Bills to create "National Tuna Week," or name a building, have an easier time than bills to provide comprehensive health or human services to low-income families. Knowing the process will not insure victory, but not knowing it makes it hard to even be a player.

Just keep reminding yourself: laws will be passed with you or without you. The choice is yours.

## WAYS TO BE HEARD

While it is true that any *individual* can be involved in the policy process, it is often easier for *groups* to have a significant impact. That is simply because of the numbers they represent (all that "butter"), and the signal they send that citizens are working for the critical 51% it takes to win.

Here are the ways to be heard:

### 1. Testimony

A legislative committee that is holding hearings can schedule 10 witnesses who represent only themselves. Or, it can schedule 10 witnesses who represent 5 organizations plus 5 coalitions – with a combined membership of several thousand voters. Since the same amount of time is involved for the legislators and the process, there is good reason for them to invite groups rather than individuals to participate.

---

**Providing testimony can be a useful way to take part in the process.**

- Testimony helps shape the debate on an issue.
- Testimony provides a written record of the various views on an issue.
- Testimony offers a legitimate way to educate the public on an issue, using the media.
- Testimony forces groups to clarify their views and present a unified position of support or opposition.
- Testimony presented at events covered by Cable Access TV reach a broader audience.

---

In order to testify at a public hearing, you may need to contact the staff of the legislative committee and ask to be considered as a witness. Or, you may just need to arrive early and sign up – that is more commonly the case in part-time or local legislatures. Sometimes staff will want a brief synopsis of your views and whom you represent, as well as any personal stake you have in the outcome.

**Note:** Preparing and presenting testimony is NOT considered lobbying by the Internal Revenue Service if you have a letter from the Committee Chair requesting the testimony and you are a nonprofit electing to come under 501(h).

**Effective testimony includes:**

- An easily understood, jargon-free, 5 -10 minute statement (3 minutes at the city or county council level), focused on the issue before the committee;

- The basic facts, including who you represent and your involvement in the issue;

- A clear statement of your points of agreement or disagreement with what is being discussed (the bill or budget item);

- Changes you would like made;

- Real examples of *who* will be affected by the matter being discussed, and *how* (concurrent media work can be especially effective here); and

- A rebuttal of the opposition's main argument(s).

Not only can testimony be used to educate the media and the decision makers, it can also be used to educate your own members, and to help clarify your position vis-à-vis other groups in the community.

When actually presenting testimony, it is essential to be ready with a short summary (with just a few highlights), because Committee hearings are often interrupted or cut short. Know the material so well that you can look Committee members in the eye rather than staring at your paper as you read. Since members may ask questions, it helps to have answers to the most likely questions prepared (and rehearsed) in advance. In some cases you can tell friendly staff some questions you would like to be asked.

## 2. Lobbying is another good way to be involved

"It is the first amendment right to petition our government."

Lobbying may be thought of as the province of cigar-chomping wheeler-dealers doling out cash, but in reality it is a more open, established part of the process. Whereas advocacy just means speaking up, lobbying (which is one form of advocacy) concerns *speaking up to convey a position to an elected official on a pending piece of legislation.* It is how everyone from paid professionals to average citizens can make their views known to decision makers about a pending or proposed change in public policy. Lobbying is a protection written into our Constitution. It is the first amendment right to "petition" our government.

It is particularly important that the nonprofit community lobby. Without their presence, the system and its policy products will likely reflect only the interests of those concerned with maximizing profits. That works against many of the activities operated by community and faith-based organizations.

Nonprofits have a right to lobby. It is written into law and regulation. The IRS published a letter in 2001 noting that nonprofits are encouraged to lobby and that it doesn't mean that the organization will face increased chances of being audited (see the IRS letter in the Appendix). Nonprofits should be encouraged to lobby and should understand that they will not be penalized for doing so.

**The object of lobbying is to bring to bear whatever power you have to influence legislators' votes, through:**

- Information and education (fact sheets, analyses, direct experience, reports);

- Numbers of constituents or people (e.g., in the hearing room, at town hall meetings);

- Use of media (to get attention, make an issue hot, enlist emotions, personalize an issue);

- Talking (Schmoozing, cajoling, discussing, persuading, negotiating)

- The influence and connections of board members.

**HELPING IN CAMPAIGNS:** Groups that are tax-exempt under 501(c)(3) of the federal tax code cannot support or oppose candidates for office. However, any individual associated with a group can work for or against candidates on their own time, if they do not use the name or resources of the group. Also these groups are permitted by law to establish other types of nonprofits that are permitted to support or oppose candidates.

The object is not to be liked, but to be respected and heard. At the heart of the process is the perception of power – who has it, how it is wielded, who wins, who loses. Money is not necessary to convey power; commitment, persistence, voters, the ability to attract the media – all are forms of power available to advocates.

One way to get involved in lobbying is to hire a professional to represent your group (on a part-time contract basis, or full-time as a member of your staff) with the legislature. But even the hired guns need to show that real voters and taxpayers stand behind them. It is increasingly common for legislators and members of Congress to say they will not meet with a lobbyist unless constituents from the district are present, or to always give priority to "real people", a.k.a. voters, over lobbyists. *Personal lobbying is one of the best ways to be effective in the political arena.*

### Know Your State

Being an effective advocate means different things in different states. Only 9 state legislatures are full-time; a few meet every other year. If your state has a very short legislative session (6-12 weeks each year), then it may be critical to have a good, on-going relationship with the people who work in the Governor's office or executive branch agencies. A mental health advocate in Louisiana said, "I spend very little time at the legislature. If my items are not included in the Governor's budget, there simply is not time to get them included once the legislature convenes." To advocates in a state with a year-long legislative session, that approach would not make sense. You need to know the peculiarities of your state. Spending time with more experienced advocates and getting on the mailing list of a good advocacy organization are good ways to learn.

Virtually every governmental entity has a web site that explains how it works and how its staff or elected officials can be contacted. Many are listed in free pamphlets distributed by the League of Women Voters. Other good sources are: **www.ncsl.org** (for the web site of your state legislature), **http://thomas.loc.gov** (legislative information from The Library of Congress), and **www.house.gov** (for the U.S. Congress).

**Effective lobbying includes:**

- Marshalling expertise (including stories of individuals who will be affected);

- Keeping track of relevant legislation;

- Paying attention to Committee votes (which are sometimes *not* published);

- Working with other lobbyists;

- Getting to know the staff (including the secretary's name);

- Educating others (including friendly legislators);

- Training others how to lobby and get involved.

**SPECIAL TIPS** Experienced lobbyists add: wear comfortable shoes, and always leave a paper trail, something in writing to show that you were there – like a fact sheet or simple note, with your name, address, e-mail address, and/or telephone number.

And *never* be disappointed at meeting with staff instead of a legislator. They have a lot of influence with their bosses, know the issues, and do much of the work.

### 3. Reaching Other Voters, the Media

**Each of these basic tools can easily be adapted to reach those other key audiences: other voters and the media.**

- A letter to your state Senator can be re-written as a blog post, or a letter to the editor of your local newspaper. If it is published, you will be reaching other voters; even if it is not published you are calling attention to your issue (and point of view) to the opinion-shapers at the newspaper.

- The same message you convey in a call to your Representative's office can be relayed to the audience of a radio call-in show. You will be reaching other voters via the airwaves, and also alerting the station's programmers of listener interest in your issue.

- The reasons you give a legislator for supporting a bill could be repeated at an adult Sunday school class or PTA meeting... and written up for their newsletters.

In each case you will be informing other voters and the local media. And do not be discouraged if you do not get on the air or in print in the major media. It helps to remember that "media" just means, a means of communicating. That includes countless less formal ways to reach other people: apartment house bulletin boards, congregation or professional newsletters, Facebook, blogs, e-mail lists, posters, flyers, skits, bumper stickers....

### Two Additional Tips

One Texas legislator commented that consciously or not, most legislators are looking for issues that are win-win. By that he meant: the legislator wins when the proposal is introduced, through favorable media attention and the approval of other voters and then wins again at campaign time, because the supporters of the bill show up to help answer phones, contribute money, put signs on their lawns, and generally help with re-election. (If a nonprofit is classified as a 501(c)(3) by the IRS it cannot take part in campaign activities. But individuals can always be active in campaigns if they are not representing a 501(c)(3) or using the group's resources.)

Many issues important to nonprofits, by contrast, are what he described as "lose-lose". By that he meant that when the proposal is introduced the legislator loses because often there is negative (or no) media attention, and the indifference (or disapproval) of other voters. Then at campaign time the legislators lose again because the bill's supporters and beneficiaries are nowhere to be seen. If

> "If we want legislators to champion our policies, we should work to help make our issuees winners at some point."

we want legislators to champion our policies, he was saying, we should work to help make our issues winners at some point. That means we have to get them before the media, expand the voter base (e.g., by voter registration), and be willing to work on re-election campaigns of legislators who support our issues.

A Michigan state legislator made the same point another way. The decision is easy, he explained, when a legislator is asked to support something that is "good policy/good politics" – like indexing social security benefits. That was the right thing to do, and popular with voters – good policy, and also good politics.

It is equally easy to make a decision not to support something that is "bad policy/bad politics" – like designating scholarship funds for the Ku Klux Klan. That choice is equally clear.

What makes many nonprofit issues difficult to support, he explained, is that they often represent "good policy/bad politics". They may be the right choice but they are hard to support because being associated with them has negative political consequences (or no return for the effort). One of our jobs as advocates is to turn our issues into "good policy/good politics."

But getting laws passed is only one part of the process.

### 4. Commenting on a Regulation

Once a law is passed, an executive branch agency becomes responsible for carrying it out. Good advocates will birddog a law's implementation just as thoroughly as they did the legislative process.

The first step is usually drafting the regulations to govern the program. For nearly every regulation, a "Notice of Proposed Rulemaking" – NPRM - is published by the responsible government agency so the public can comment.

At the federal level, final regulations and Notices of Proposed Rulemaking, are published in a five-day-a-week publication called the *Federal Register*, which is available in all federal Depository libraries; from the local, regional, or national office of the agency affected; and on the Internet from the National Archives and Records Administration (http://www.nara.gov).

States may issue *final* regulations through a Governor, Lieutenant Governor, Attorney General's, or some other office. States also publish *proposed* regulations, but usually on a monthly or weekly basis. It is important to learn which office publishes *draft* and *final* regulations in your state, and the library or Internet sources for them. A state library, or Secretary of State's office is a good place to start.

> "Few people are likely to go visit a library or web site every week just to read through the latest government regulations, and even if they did, sometimes the regulations are hard to understand."

But few people are likely to go visit a library or web site every week just to read through the latest government regulations, and even if they did, sometimes the regulations are hard to understand. That is another reason for linking up with a good advocacy group. Advocacy groups – state and national – not only get copies of the regulations important to their issues, they analyze them, clarify them, and notify the people on their mailing lists when comment letters are needed. Best of all, they are likely to alert you to key issues to look out for, and may offer sample comment letters to get you started. But the basic process is pretty straightforward.

Each Notice includes information that makes it easy for citizens to comment: the name of the agency issuing the regulation, a summary of the action being taken, the date by which comment letters are needed, a person and telephone number to contact with any questions, where to address your comments, and an explanation of what the regulation contains.

Then the full text of the proposed regulation follows. (This part maybe less understandable because it is written to meet legal standards.)

### Comment letters should:

- Briefly describe your group, note any expertise you have (personal experience counts), and why you are interested in the proposed regulation;
- Acknowledge points you agree with, and identify points you disagree with; and
- Describe factual situations that would be affected by the regulation, and if possible, suggest alternative language.

Since each letter is counted separately, it is best to ask every member of your group to send one, rather than have a single letter with multiple signatures. Personalizing each letter also makes an impact. It also helps to send a copy of your comment letter to your senators and representatives. Increasingly agencies are taking comments via e-mail.

And if your organization is a 501(c)(3) nonprofit organization, work on regulations does not count toward the lobbying limits under federal IRS law. (However in some states, work on regulations does count as lobbying and must be disclosed – although there is no limit placed. Check the rules in your state.)

**DO NOT FORGET** At every step, policy advocacy has a role for everyone: people to write letters, make phone calls, get facts, issue reports, work with the media, develop strategy, lobby, discuss, think, show up, care. Some of that is sure to describe you.

Sometimes, local efforts are not enough. Child health offers a good example of an issue that needed a national campaign for success.

## From Good Ideas, More Grow

Advocacy ideas pop up, get adopted and adapted, and re-appear in many forms.

Consider this idea that popped up in Oklahoma. One chilly spring day a group of parents and children appeared at their state Capitol, carrying big trash bags. Faces flushed, the children were obviously excited to be there, so a friendly stranger asked what they were doing: "Are you bringing *trash* to the Capitol?" "Oh no," said one of the boys, turning to his father to ask if he could show the lady what was in the bags.

The night before, they had gathered around a table and gone to work. They took brightly colored pieces of paper, folded them in half, and then each half was folded in half again. The bottom two panels were pulled together and stapled at either end, creating a 3-sided paper tent. On one panel were the words: PAY NOW, OR PAY MORE LATER. On the other visible panel were the words: PREVENT CHILD ABUSE. On the bottom panel was their group's name, address, and contact information.

Then they divided up, a parent and a child in each pair, and fanned out to visit all the legislators' offices. At every office the child approached the receptionist and asked: "Can I put one of these on your desk?" Without fail, the receptionists' response was positive: "Did you help make that? Well you put that right where *everybody* can see it!"

Within about an hour, every office in the Oklahoma State Legislature had a brightly colored reminder that if we do not "pay now" to prevent child abuse, we will all "pay later." And Capitol occupants could be heard throughout the day, commenting on the families and their simple message. ("Did you see those children? Now, who could be *for* child abuse?!")

Paper tents are an easy, low cost way to call attention to an issue, while teaching newcomers that this is their Capitol, a place where any one of any age can help be a voice for those who need one. Although simple, they can even play a role in a sophisticated national campaign.

Hearing about those paper tents inspired a health educator eager to direct some of her state's tobacco settlement dollars toward tobacco cessation. She rounded up more recruits (the widow of a man who died of lung cancer, a public health nurse, a PTA member and some high school students) and together they made the nearly 3-hour trip to their Capitol. The night before they used ordinary copy paper, rolled to form paper "cigarettes" (complete with paper ash at one end) for every legislator. Along the sides were key facts about the harm tobacco does to young bodies. The finished "cigarettes" and accompanying Fact Sheets were loaded into trash bags, for easy carrying.

Her report, written to her county's Tobacco Free group, concluded with the following:

> Our mission for the day was to deliver butts and fact sheets to all 147 legislators and Governor, and to meet with as many legislators as possible, including our own (who used to smoke 3 packs of cigarettes a day).

> Despite not eating lunch, being on our feet all day, and having only seconds to spare between deliveries, we did make press! A Press Intern for The Herald wrote a story on us! She interviewed

*each of us and even sat in on one group visit.*

*All in all it was a grand success. We learned! We exercised! We met new people! We met with six Senators and four Representatives! We delivered all butts and fact sheets! And best of all, we stressed the importance of tobacco prevention and control in our state! Remember that the session is not over yet! The most challenging part is yet to come.*

POST-SCRIPT: letters, calls, e-mails, and more visits followed. Together with the efforts of other advocates, they succeeded in winning tobacco settlement dollars for tobacco cessation.

By fall of that same year, these tobacco free advocates were already busy hosting meetings in the community and reserving a room in the Capitol for a second annual lobby/education day in their Capitol. Learning about the paper tents had given them the courage to take the first step, which led to next steps, and before long the kind of solid, effective, year-round advocacy that gets results.

# Taking Part in a National Campaign

For years, local child advocates struggled to find health care for children from families with no health coverage. Individual stories would occasionally make the news, inspire sympathy, and generate the needed care, but each individual case took prodigious efforts, and left millions more – nearly 11 million by 1997 – without coverage. Meanwhile, advocates were also working hard to win expanded coverage under Medicaid – a strategy that worked least well for the children in the poorest states, and required massive efforts by groups with tiny staffs and shoestring budgets.

Frustrated, advocates requested a meeting with President Clinton's health policy staff. In December of 1996, just about the time decisions on the next year's budget were being decided, thirty advocates went to the White House. Each represented an organization directly involved in maternal and child health – everyone from the Children's Defense Fund and the The Arc to the March of Dimes and Children's Hospitals. Their plea was simple: put money in the budget to cover uninsured children. When the President's budget proposals went to the Congress a few months later, there was some money, but the amount was disappointingly small.

Lacking robust help from the White House, the advocacy groups turned to *Congress*, and by March two senior U.S. Senators had agreed to introduce a bill to create a new Child Health Insurance Program, or CHIP: Republican Orin Hatch, of Utah, and Democrat Ted Kennedy, of Massachusetts. In the House of Representatives another bi-partisan pair of champions was found: Republican Nancy Johnson of Connecticut, and Democrat Robert Matsui of California.

Some of the more traditional health groups balked at joining the effort – a few regarded it as a hopeless case, others disagreed over how it might be funded. Ironically, that problem proved to be an advantage because it forced supporters to look for new allies. Before long they had enlisted groups that cared about children but were not necessarily identified with health (PTA's, and school administrators), groups that worked on adult health issues (the American Cancer Society, the American Heart Association), and a growing list of other odd couples (e.g., business groups and sororities, the American Muslim Council and the National Black Police Association). Every week support grew broader, and deeper.

In a parallel effort the state Attorneys General of nearly 40 states were already suing the tobacco industry for the costs of tobacco-related medical care, and calling attention to the harm that tobacco does to children's health. That spring, the first big tobacco settlement was reached with the states, and the idea that tobacco was bad for children seemed to be on everyone's lips. Suddenly the idea of funding CHIP with proceeds from a tobacco tax looked winnable.

At the same time advocates worked with the *media:* scheduling meetings with editorial boards, giving background information to journalists, and writing commentaries that began appearing in local newspapers everywhere, and spreading the word through countless newsletters.

"Ultimately, the Campaign for Child Health Now included over 200 national and state organizations from across the political spectrum and the U.S."

Plus, they used the Internet to activate *grassroots networks* of potential supporters all across the country. (By modern standards this was a primitive internet organizing effort, with the various campaign partners simply feeding their e-mail address lists to "...this guy at a computer, creating an internet tree..." according to one participant.) Ultimately, the Campaign for Child Health Now included over 200 national and state organizations from across the political spectrum and the U.S. - all of them spreading the word and informing their members. They kept the pressure on their members of Congress, and the White House.

Two more breakthroughs provided momentum. In June the tobacco industry agreed to a massive $368 billion, multi-year settlement with the states – at least part of which could be used for child health. A few weeks later the White House and Congressional leaders reached agreement on a budget, including authority for CHIP. Advocates still had to work to make sure the various agreements did not unravel, but by early August of 1997, legislation authorizing CHIP had been passed and signed into law.

It remained for each state legislature to design the version of CHIP that would make the most sense for them. That fall, just about one year from the initial meeting at the White House, California and Connecticut became two of the earliest states to pass their own enabling legislation, and start drawing on the $24 billion federal CHIP dollars available to provide health insurance for children from low-earning families. Two years later, Texas was the last state to act, when a reluctant Governor George Bush signed the Texas version of CHIP into law.

Those advocates in the *Campaign for Child Health Now* did many things right: they pressed ahead when others thought they could not win, they built on already-established relationships with elected officials, they seized opportunities, they organized beyond the usual suspects to create a politically powerful coalition, and they made sure all three legs of the advocacy stool were firmly in place.

Today millions of children have health coverage who would not have it otherwise, and more than a dozen web sites provide up-to-date information for local advocates working to make CHIP available to eligible children in their states.

If you think legislative victories are only won by powerful lobbyists wandering the halls of Congress, writing big campaign checks and throwing lavish parties, think again. The campaign for CHIP is proof once again that our democratic system still works. Those billions in the budget were not a payoff for fancy parties; they are there because of good old-fashioned hard work and grassroots organizing. And everyone who spoke up, wrote a letter, signed a card, made a call, contributed money, questioned a candidate, or raised the issue at a community event, played a part. That is how democracy works.

Before any national campaign is over, it involves everyone from super-sophisticated D.C.-based lobbyists who arrange White House meetings, to absolute beginners writing their first letter or making their first phone call. They do not always win, but in this case they won big-time – and every year children everywhere win again.

As you are by now quite aware, getting a law passed by Congress is only one stage in the process, and it is a process that must be re-engaged every few years, along with annual battles over funding. In the case of CHIP, advocates who worked to get the federal law passed, then had to work with their state legislatures for a bill to adapt and carry out the federal law in their own state. After that the actual implementation of the law has to be monitored. Even as this is written, children's advocates are serving on local CHIP committees, planning the next CHIP event, inviting their state legislators and Members of Congress to visit their hospitals and clinics to meet with the families helped by CHIP, and keeping one another informed as each new step unfolds.

Being a good citizen is a bit like being a good parent: the job may change, but it never really ends.

# PART 03

# Getting Started

Once you are persuaded that more people need to be involved in advocacy and you have reminded yourself how the policy process works, it is time to start. It would be great if there were some easy rule to apply in deciding which issues to take on, and how to go about winning them, but unfortunately, there is no magic formula.

However there is a lot of useful advice around. It draws from a combination of common sense and the experience of an increasingly effective advocacy community.

The first piece of advice as you are getting started is simple. Remember that as a general rule, anything involving major change, significant costs, or controversy, will be relatively more time-consuming and difficult to achieve. Similarly, it is generally the case that anything involving only modest (or incremental) change, little or no cost, and a minimum of controversy, will be relatively easier to achieve. Either way, the size and complexity of the advocacy tasks have to be compared with the size and complexity of the resources you and your group can bring to bear. (That is not an argument for avoiding big issues, just a quick reality check.)

The next piece of advice is equally straightforward: think. Any time you take to think through your issues, your goals, and your capabilities, will always be time well spent. An ill-considered effort can cost your group more than just disappointment. It can reflect poorly on your organization, demoralize your members, and may even establish bad precedents. A carefully considered effort will provide useful lessons whatever the outcome.

Now, just in case you or your colleagues are new to advocacy, or have not done much policy advocacy in a while, here is an Advocacy Fitness Plan – with low impact, medium impact and high impact exercises – to get you in shape. (Like the material in the Appendix section of this guide, this Advocacy Fitness Plan can be copied and used as a handout at future gatherings.)

## An Advocacy Fitness Plan

Becoming politically fit is a lot like becoming physically fit. Team sports and exercise classes have their place, but sometimes it is just you and the TV – and nothing you can do about it. Even if others are theoretically available to run or shoot baskets, they may not be available on the same schedule. One way or another, being on your own (living in a rural area, leading a busy life, or just being shy) is no reason not to keep your advocacy fitness level high.

Physical fitness is a useful analogy to keep in mind for another reason. Just as your flesh-and-blood muscles need regular use, and increased activity over time, so do your political muscles. Stop using them altogether and you will quickly become politically flabby; use them regularly and your level of advocacy fitness will soar.

So, what follows is a quick and easy, 10-step advocacy fitness plan, a kind of aerobics for advocates. And, like those aerobics workouts on early morning TV, it has three levels: low, medium and high impact (impact on you, that is, not on your issue or cause).

## LEVEL 1

*Low Impact – Every month do at least one of the following:*

### 1. Get on the mailing list of an advocacy group that focuses on an issue you care about.

> "Joining a group is good because it supports advocacy efforts monetarily. But just getting on an e-mail list is free."

Joining a group is good because it supports advocacy efforts monetarily (usual annual costs run between $10 and $40). But just getting on an e-mail list is free. At the same time, you will become better informed about the issue. They'll tell you when your voice is needed, and supply a sample message you can personalize.

### 2. Enlist a friend.

Get someone you know interested in your issue and excited enough to do something – anything – about it (learning more counts, as does attending a meeting or showing up to volunteer on a one-time basis). Do not worry about what they do; once hooked they will figure out for themselves what is most comfortable.

### 3. Inform a stranger.

You can have an impact just by carrying on a conversation in a place where others are sure to hear: the subway, a checkout line, or elevator. You could post a Fact Sheet on the bulletin board in your apartment complex or local grocery store, put an informative bumper sticker on your car, or post something on a computer bulletin board for other subscribers to read. Or, you could ask that a group you belong to (E.g., Rotary Club, church, mosque, or synagogue, PTA, professional association) consider forming a task force on the issue you care most about.

This level is like the exercises where your feet do not leave the floor and your movements are quite gentle. But even if you get no farther than Level I, by the end of a year you will be better informed, and will have gotten a few more people thinking about others in your community.

## LEVEL 2

### *Medium Impact –Every week do at least one of the following:*

### 4. Write a policy-maker (federal, state or local).

Practice what you already know; exercise those political muscles. Once you have done it a few times, it will get easier. As with most things in life, the first time is usually the hardest. If your elected officials like getting messages by e-mail, use it.

### 5. Call a policy-maker (federal, state, or local).

Ditto. It helps that U.S. Senators and Representatives all have local offices with local telephone numbers, and some have toll-free lines as well. You may find yourself talking to a machine, but that is easier for some people, and your message will be conveyed.

### 6. Visit a policy-maker (federal, state, or local).

Ditto again. It is not enough to read about making a visit; sooner or later you need to use what you learned. Try it, you may like it. Those who start out feeling the most timid, the most reluctant, frequently turn out to be the best converts once they try. Sometimes novice lobbyists use words like "seductive," "addictive," and "intoxicating," to describe the experience.

This level is comparable to those exercises where the body movements are more energetic, the pace is faster, and a lot more bending and stretching is involved. But the impact can also be far more dramatic. If everyone who claimed to care about others wrote, called, or visited a policy-maker every week, their issues would fare very differently in the political process. So long as most of the people who claim to be concerned keep their concern to themselves, social issues/the environment/the arts will continue to get only a fraction of the public dollars and political attention afforded to just about everything else.

## LEVEL 3

### *High Impact –Every week, in addition, do at least one of the following:*

### 7. 8. 9. Write, call, or visit other voters.

Every week, automatically re-cast your letters, calls, and visits for use with a larger audience: the voting public. Every time you write, call, or visit a policy-maker, think of a way to get the same message across to other voters. Re-write the letter to your legislator as a letter-to-the-editor; call a radio call-in show with the message you left on your council member's message machine; repeat what you said to the mayor at the Rotary Club or with your exercise group. That way you will double (or triple) your impact with only a fraction more investment of energy and time.

This level is like the exercise routine where you jump up and down, fling out your arms and legs, and quickly work up a sweat. At this point you will be a true citizen activist, with advocacy muscles that are taut and working at their peak. Go for it.

## BONUS POINTS

### 10. Work for a visionary goal.

While every effort counts, groups still have a greater chance of success than individuals working on their own. That said, even very effective groups can sometimes get so caught up in responding on an immediate, practical level that they lose perspective. It is essential, as the old civil rights refrain goes, to "keep your eyes on the prize."

So, for the greatest impact, join with the advocacy group of your choice to work for at least one visionary goal. It is important for people organizing food drives to think of ending poverty, not just alleviating hunger; important that domestic violence advocates work toward creating a less-violent society, even as they fight for increasing the sensitivity of police, or expanding shelter capacity.

Management objectives, organization charts, and inter-agency agreements all have their place, but good advocates must never forget that a better world, not the next annual report, is what these efforts are all about.

> "A better world, not the next annual report, is what these efforts are all about."

## SIX CRITICAL STEPS

Conditions will vary from place to place, but a 5-10 person committee is usually a good place to start. (It helps if each is already part of a group or network that might be activated.) Sometimes they will come together out of a shared concern, or because they are looking for new ways to be effective against old problems. Other times you will find yourself drafting people.

Once they are assembled, you will need a plan. When it comes to working out an advocacy plan, there are probably as many formulas as there are advocates, but most include the following ingredients in some form or other.

### Identify your issue, and goal(s).

A *problem* is a cause for concern, a matter needing action. Elder abuse is a problem.

An *issue* is just the problem framed as something you can do something about. For example, you may determine that elder abuse often goes unreported in your community because the people who care for vulnerable elderly are not taught how to identify the signs of abuse and thus do not report. "Elder abuse" is very broad and hard to organize around, but "a campaign to improve reporting through training" sounds do-able. An issue always contains a solution or partial solution; it affects people, is specific, and theoretically winnable.

Your *goal* is what you specifically hope to accomplish, the objective toward which your advocacy efforts are directed. Ending all abuse of the elderly – physical, emotional, financial, psychological – is a laudable long-term goal, but it is too sweeping for most groups to build an advocacy plan around. For starters, few could command the resources required, or even know where to begin.

Convincing the legislature to require - and fund - the training to increase accurate reporting by caregivers, on the other hand, is a narrower goal, but it is one that could help many vulnerable older people. Moreover, it is specific enough to build a plan around (with short and long-term goals) and possibly win – and it is consistent with the long-term goal. From an advocacy perspective that makes it a better choice. (You will save yourself a lot of grief if, early on, you define your issue and goals as clearly and specifically as possible, and relate both to your resources.)

## Be accountable and representative.

As you plan, it is important to be sure you represent those you are speaking for, and not just your own ideas of what is needed. Good advocates – like the tobacco free group that included the widows of long-time smokers and teens tempted to smoke – do. What their constituents wished is what they pursued. Nobody likes to be spoken for without being consulted.

This is something every good advocate grapples with; it is especially sensitive if the people involved are mentally competent but frightened and overwhelmed (for example, someone who is just been diagnosed as HIV-positive), or unable to speak for themselves (developmentally delayed infants or adults with dementia).

Who can speak for them? One answer is to rely on surrogates, like family members or a group whose members are similarly affected. A good test is to ask whom *you* would want as your advocate under similar circumstances – a doctor? your family? a court-appointed ethicist? an advocacy group? your peers? And what if you were just unsure how the policy process works – would that give someone else the right to speak for you? *This is one issue you have to think through carefully, and plan for, in advance.*

## Get the facts.

There are few worse advocates than people with good intentions and bad information. Good advocacy plans are based on solid facts, not anecdotes, guesses, or whatever happened to make it into the media. A first discussion of elder abuse may reveal that some think the most pressing concern is a failure of police to respond when abuse is suspected (not the failure of caregivers to make reports), while others believe the real issue is unregulated businesses that prey on the elderly. Fail to get the facts first, and you may find yourself organizing around the wrong issue.

It is easy to assume the worst (about the mental health system, government bureaucrats, local schools), based on an anecdote or two. As a *Washington Post* editorial noted so succinctly: "… the plural of anecdote is not data." A quick fact-finding effort can help establish whether the anecdotes are the exception or part of a pattern.

It is also important to establish where you need to intervene to alleviate the problem. It will not help to complain to your United States Senator about under-reporting elder abuse; that is a responsibility of local agencies. Nor does it help to fuss at state legislators over whether nicotine may be treated as a controlled substance – which is a federal responsibility.

Make a checklist of what you need to know to proceed, and make assignments for getting it. Collecting information about a problem or its possible solution is not all drudgery. It can be a good way to get your volunteers invested in an issue, and fact-finding is something even shy people can do.

Getting the facts may require some research, a focus group, or survey of your own, but there is a staggering amount of information already available. Try that route first. There are studies, reports, surveys, planning documents, testimony, task force proposals and commission recommendations on a myriad of topics. They are available from state legislatures, government agencies at every level, universities, public libraries, and in the files of countless nonprofit groups. Librarians are a great potential resource.

Local advocates and chapters of national groups are another good place to start (for example, your state's chapter of the American Cancer Society would have good statistics related to children and smoking in your state, and the state chapter of the AARP would have good information on needs and services related to the elderly), as are state chapters of professional organizations (the American Public Health Association or the National Association of Social Workers).

And today, anyone with access to a computer will find a world of information available on the World Wide Web.

### Develop a strategy.

Once you have got your issue clearly defined, and you have learned as much as you can about the problem – including who is responsible for it, it is time to map out a strategy.

Advocates spend a lot of time reacting to others, but good advocates are pro-active as well. Both require a *strategy* – an overall approach, an action plan.

Framing the issue one way or another is a critical step. Framing the elder abuse issue as a need for caretakers to be trained in better reporting helps determine your strategy – in this case, a campaign to win a law to require training – along with necessary funding. In this case the overall strategy is *legislative*.

If the issue had been framed as a need for better public understanding of the problem, you would pursue an *educational* strategy; if individual elderly were denied protections already afforded by law, you might pursue a *legal* strategy through the courts; if there is already a law but the regulations to carry it out are inadequate, you would pursue an *administrative* strategy; and if there is a requirement in the law that just is not being funded, your strategy might be *budgetary*.

> "Developing an advocacy strategy is a lot like the process you would go through to organize a fundraiser or put on a show."

Developing an advocacy strategy is a lot like the process you would go through to organize a fundraiser or put on a show. You would draw up a plan, set some interim goals, and make a calendar with deadlines for achieving them. You would make lists; think through who is good at what; get a good committee; and recruit volunteers for the other jobs needing to be done. Early on you would figure out how much you can spend, where it will come from, and who will be responsible for the practical details – like budgets, signing correspondence, keeping records.

As you develop your advocacy strategy, be honest about your capacities. Suing the department responsible for elder abuse might seem appealing, but it is a costly strategy that requires a large budget, attorneys on staff, or attorneys willing to work for free. You need to consider the personnel and dollars required for various strategies, as well as how long they would take before showing results. A small group that is new to advocacy might do better to begin with something time-limited and very specific, whereas a group with well-established community ties and an experienced staff could consider something more ambitious and long-lasting. (Working in coalitions is one way to include elements of both.)

Think through what you can do alone, and also what kind of help you might recruit if that is what is needed. (See the end of Part V: Advocacy Readiness Checklist.)

Finally, you need to consider the less tangible but ever-so-critical matter of style. The Grey Panthers and the Junior League both care about elder abuse, but their styles in approaching the issue will be different. Your advocacy efforts reflect on you and your group; plan your strategy accordingly.

## Get to know the decision-makers and their staff.

Knowing the players is not just a matter of being able to list their names.

Decision-makers are like anybody else: they do not like to be approached only when you want something, and they are appreciative if you take the time to understand the constraints they face. It always helps to recognize their needs. In your own time: offer to do research, help in a campaign, pitch in when they need extra hands. It will not go unnoticed. Effective advocates cultivate relationships with decision-makers and their staffs over a long period of time, and understand the process well enough to know when to ask for something (or not). You should not try to get a bill introduced at the end of a session, for example, or seek funding for a project after the budget has been set.

Getting to know the decision-makers has another clear advantage: it teaches who has what kinds of power at varying levels of government, so you will not be asking for things they cannot deliver.

For years, a statewide Human Services Coalition in Utah held monthly meetings with key staff from the Department of Health and Human Services. Over the years those Friday afternoon sessions provided an effective form of feedback about program operation to the policy makers. But they also offered a way for advocates and policy makers to get to know one another in a collegial and non-adversarial setting, while learning what different staff can – and cannot – do. This is not about getting chummy, and it will not guarantee agreement on the issues. But it is a key element of developing mutual respect for all concerned.

## Broaden your base of support.

Senior organizations may be the logical place to start if you are trying to improve elder abuse reporting, but younger relatives also feel outraged by elder abuse and many people would be interested in policies to protect their grandparents. So might public health professionals, faith communities, academic gerontologists, or veterans. These are all likely allies.

But others are also concerned – like local merchants with elderly customers or the police officers who get called to investigate. These are your unlikely allies– and they can be very important. Think how striking it is when insurance executives join forces with consumer groups to press for better health care policies, when loggers join forces with environmentalists, or when sheriffs testify in support of domestic violence shelters. Alliances like that are striking because they are unexpected, and signal that voter support is broader than previously supposed.

At some point you might wish to form or join a bigger coalition, so that is discussed in the next section. For now it is enough to note that in the world of public policy, success often depends on being able to show a broad range of support (lots of "butter"), and an absence – or neutrality – of the likely opposition.

You have gathered your information. You have developed a personal citizenship fitness plan. Now it is time to think once again in terms of your group.

## WHO ELSE TO INVOLVE

> "In politics there are two rules – Rule #1 is: nothing happens overnight; and Rule #2 is: you cannot change Rule #1. "

As you think about whom to involve in advocacy, you may be thinking about people with lobbying experience, or those who are known for having strong opinions. They should be included, but you will miss a lot of talent if you stop there. In politics there are two rules – Rule #1 is: nothing happens overnight; and Rule #2 is: you cannot change Rule #1.

### So when you think about the traits that produce good advocates, look for perseverance.

Good advocates, it is often said, can always be recognized by their running shoes: they are the marathon types who pace themselves and never give up.

### Next, look for a couple of noodges, sticklers for detail.

A lot of advocacy turns on small details and basic courtesies, like thanking every city council member who supports your position, or following up meetings with state legislators with a personal note. Those details count: that is why many politicians try to add brief personal notes to the form letters sent out by their staff.

### A third trait to look for is passion.

That is not the same as volume or drama – it is possible to feel passionately about something while speaking softly and working quietly. Think of all the times you have seen an issue pushed to the forefront by someone directly involved – a student who survived a gun attack, relatives of someone killed by a drunk driver, persons with a physical or mental disability, victims of domestic violence. They are not policy experts or professional lobbyists, but they know their issue first-hand, as family members, victims, or service consumers. This is not a job for them; all too often it *is* a matter of life or death.

### Fourth, seek modesty, people who do not need the spotlight.

You can accomplish a lot in politics, the old saying goes, if you do not care who gets the credit. Often the advocates are working behind the scenes doing the legwork, making the phone calls, drafting the speeches and letters-to-the-editor while the elected officials are getting their pictures in the paper and the plaques on their walls. Some of the best advocacy is felt rather than seen.

### And do not be afraid to start small.

That is normal. It would be great if half the people in your group wanted to join in your advocacy effort from the start, but that is neither likely nor necessary. Most advocacy efforts begin with, and are sustained by, small groups of dedicated people. You do not have to start with big numbers; you do need to start with big commitment. That, not quantity, is what counts:

- One grieving mother started M.A.D.D.

- Two people – one English, one African – started the movement to free poor nations from debt.

- A handful of (mostly young) environmentalists started Earth Day.

Sociologist Aldon Morris notes that only about 10-15% of the population sustained the civil rights movement. Others note that in any self-interested group about 5% can be counted on to be activists. That is not surprising. There is never a time when most people are counted as activists, nor is that needed. What is needed is a core group of people serving as catalysts; they will do the detail work and infuse other people with their passion.

Your job is to find and cultivate your group's 10%: the people needed to sustain the efforts over the long haul.

---

### A Special Word About Boards

There is a tendency in the nonprofit world to think of a Board of Directors in terms of their ability to raise money, look good on a letterhead, and/or offer expert advice. That is not bad, it is just shortsighted. Nonprofit board members' greatest assets may be their access to decision-makers, their credibility in the broader community, and their power —all of which can be harnessed on behalf of the agency's mission and clientele. Board members often have an easier time getting appointments with legislators or a Governor's staff person, and are likely to know other community leaders.

Every nonprofit board should have an advocacy plan of its own, to spell out the ways the board will act as advocates for the group and its members. Board members can educate their peers in the community, work with the media, help deflect community fears, organize public forums,

> **Board members often have an easier time getting appointments with legislators**

testify, and lobby. In addition, they can make the case that nonprofit groups represent jobs and income to their communities, as well as valuable services. That alone is a form of power, but one that is too often overlooked. For a time the Oklahoma legislature was allocating more money per capita to nonprofit youth-serving groups than any other legislature in the country. That became true after the groups began requiring that all new board members be willing to lobby on behalf of their programs and their young people. Potential board members who felt uncomfortable with the requirement were helped to find service on some other board.

## DO NOT FORGET

Even though there is much about advocacy that is common to many other undertakings, there are a few special things worth keeping in mind.

■ Whatever your long-term goal, try to build in an early, easy victory that is related to it. Nothing motivates like success and nothing discourages like inaction. Since advocacy efforts often move slowly, it helps to involve your fledgling group in anything that is consistent with your larger goals and likely to happen (or easy to win) – a small victory, but a victory. They will share some of the credit, and be more willing to press on.

■ Sort out which parts of your goal need government action and which can be accomplished without it. The strategies and personnel involved in each are often different, and the two should not be confused. Besides, elected officials do not like being asked for help that is available through the private sector, and vice versa.

■ Expect to compromise. Evelyn Burns, who taught for many years at Columbia University, used to remind her students that compromise is part of politics; the trick comes in knowing when a compromise is acceptable. A small version of something good was usually all right, she argued, because you could always build on it in the future. But it is never good to agree to institutionalize something bad; once begun, bad practice is hard to stop.

■ Remember what motivates you. Some advocates have a tendency to cite one terrible statistic after another, piling up every grim possibility imaginable. You will need facts to be credible, but people are rarely moved by statistics, no matter how dramatic they may be. Michael Harrington, a great anti-poverty advocate, once wrote, "a fact can be rationalized and explained away; an indignity cannot."

■ Humanize your facts. Talk about people you know, not faceless categories. Hardly anyone would say "yes" to helping a statistic, but the reverse is also true – most people have a hard time denying help to someone they feel they know.

■ And never forget to point out the good that will be accomplished; beating policy-makers up with bad news is more likely to paralyze than persuade.

What moves people is not just grim statistics but "a cocktail of fear and hope". The bad news may all be true, but good advocates offer policy-makers and fellow-citizens the hope that something can be done to turn it around.

## SUCCESSFUL TECHNIQUES

As you may already have guessed, all through this manual you have been learning effective techniques to adapt for use in your own advocacy efforts. They have three broad purposes.

### To Inform

You can use the Advocacy Quiz at the beginning of Part I to help others understand how natural it is to be engaging in advocacy. Use it when conducting a workshop on advocacy, or when trying to get others to join your advocacy efforts.

"Gimmicks generally do not work on their own, but they can be very effective as part of a larger, well-considered strategy."

An easy variant on that idea is to develop a different sort of quiz, one based on the most common misperceptions of your issue. When you do presentations to community groups on your issue (as compared with presentations on advocacy), begin by having the audience take The Quiz, and then discuss the answers. If you want to develop materials to accompany your talk, you might consider the format used in a New York State pamphlet which began: "In 1492 everyone *knew* the world was flat. In 1917 everyone *knew* the Titanic was unsinkable." "Today," you might continue, "everyone *knows*...[and here you fill in a myth related to your issue]." "Myths die hard [insert the correct information here]."

### To Get Action

If plans are already underway and legislation is already pending, but the legislators just are not paying much attention, you might try to devise an attention-getting gimmick like the ones described throughout this manual (for example, using Take Five Tables, or delivering paper cigarettes). Gimmicks generally do not work on their own, but they can be very effective as part of a larger, well-considered strategy.

One February a family planning group in New Hampshire followed up some of its public education efforts by sending every state legislator a valentine. It contained the results of a statewide poll showing widespread citizen support for family planning. They described their mailing as "linking romance with responsibility", but they were also making an important political point. By calling the legislators' attention to public support for this once-controversial service, they were able to win the necessary funds.

### To Win Policy Changes

A well-established group could decide to set up a *legislative network*. The Florida Nurses Association built one by identifying a current or retired nurse in each state Legislative and congressional district who would be willing to work on legislative issues important to nurses. They agreed to contact their legislators, offer to be a resource and respond to health-related questions, and get other nurses in their area to do the same.

Similarly, many groups around the country have formed CANs (e.g., a Children's Action Network, a Congregation Action Network). Organizers in one state began with just a few dozen congregations and eventually had a few hundred. Each congregation had a coordinator who agreed to be the conduit for all legislative alerts and related activity. Coordinators agree to recruit members to be part of the network, and to generate 5-15 calls or letters on a limited number of issues (no more than five) while the state legislature is in session. When that ends, CAN coordinators agree to do the same for 1 or 2 issues pending before the U.S. Congress.

The Children's Action Network in one mid-size state began in 1998, had about 1,000 members by the end of 1999, and 3,300 by the end of year 2000. A chart on their wall showing the CAN numbers by County is updated regularly. CAN members pledge to "speak up for kids" during the state legislative session: they promise to read a weekly legislative alert, and "take five" (minutes) for kids each week by contacting a policy maker with the message for that week.

Yet another network revolves around two large public meetings each year that have grown to attract several hundred local advocates, their local and state legislators, and the local media. The forums are designed to put key decision-makers together with voters twice: in the fall when the next year's budget is being developed, and again in the spring when the budget is being voted on.

Each of these legislative networks has some common elements. The expectations of participants are time-limited and relatively modest (for example, 5-15 calls or letters on a limited number of issues; 5 minutes/week; two public events). There is a staff person whose duties include nurturing the key contacts in the legislative network, and devoting time to them: answering their questions, helping them get what they need to be effective. In each case sample materials are prepared to make network participating easier – sample e-mails/letters, sample telephone scripts, sample fact sheets and issue papers.

Developing a legislative network is not a one-shot, or short-term effort. It requires knowledge and a degree of political sophistication, as well as an on-going commitment to advocacy. But it is within the reach of most organizations that follow policy issues, and it should be within the capabilities of any statewide coalition (e.g., on environmental or women's issues, the arts or human services). Ambitious advocates might combine several models. They could ask churches, mosques, and synagogues to provide the calls and letters (since they meet weekly), while depending on organizations with quarterly or annual meetings to arrange for citizen/decision-maker forums.

However, whether as an individual or as part of a group, it helps to remember: good advocacy does not always take money or sophistication, but it does take creativity and thought to come up with something that a lot of people can participate in, and that have the desired effect.

Across the country, people with shoestring operations and political novices filling their ranks, are making up in commitment and creativity for what they lack in money and sophistication. And they are pulling off minor miracles – changing laws and budgets, winning better policies for vulnerable people and causes. You can be part of that. All you need to do is try.

PART
04

# Nuts & Bolts

You've got your issue, you have put together a committee, you have drawn up your strategy (ready to be revised as needed), and you have reminded yourself how the process works.

Now it is time for the practical details, the nuts and bolts of serious policy advocacy: building coalitions, testifying, lobbying, and becoming part of the process.

Take a deep breath. Here we go.

## Building Coalitions, Broadening Your Base

**A coalition is an organization of organizations.** Coalitions are not just lists of individuals; they represent the combined influence and support of multiple organizations – each of which may have dozens or hundreds of members.

The most obvious reason for building a coalition is to increase your numbers. But there is a subtler reason as well. Life often feels hectic, disjointed, or too busy. Modern communities are full of families with busy lives and no close relatives living near by. That proves especially hard when tragedy or trouble strikes. It also takes a toll on the neighbors and friends who would like to help but are not sure how to get involved.

If public policies are involved, coalitions offer a way. They can provide a means for communities to come together, to learn about common problems, and set some priorities for policies of mutual benefit to everyone. And because they represent bigger numbers, there are more people to share the work. One small group, or working people with limited time to give, will not have to do everything.

Coalitions are particularly well suited to advocacy strategies. They show a commitment to think ahead, anticipate alternatives, and achieve political results.

**State and local coalitions:**

- Combine community resources;
- Offer a forum for thinking about community problems;
- Reduce competition for funding and volunteer time;

- Provide an efficient way to work with community organizations; and
- Offer support and expertise to small groups, as well as a network for families with special needs.

By working through coalitions, your group can do more than you could do on your own. Three steps will get you started.

## 1. IDENTIFY A CONVENER AND LIKELY COALITION MEMBERS

You may want to be the convener – calling others to join in with you, or you might consider whether there are other groups with more experience, community standing, or staff (for setting up meetings, keeping notes) that would be better suited to the role.

The committee you have formed should help decide who should convene the coalition, and which groups are likely to be potential coalition members. It also helps to decide on basic principles that all coalition members must support. That way, organizations with wildly different goals or approaches will decline to join – and you will not be in the position of telling some group you do not want them.

First, use your committee to list all your *likely allies,* every group with an obvious interest in the issue at hand. One idea will lead to another: once someone mentions one faith or professional group, others in the same general category will spring to mind.

Once you have listed all the likely allies, next think of some groups that are not so obvious, some *odd couples,* or *unlikely allies.* You will not need (or get) as many of these, but you do not need as many: having even a few odd couples sends a political signal that you are reaching out and talking to more than others who already agree with you.

Then, as you consider who should approach each of the groups about joining your coalition, keep in mind something known to all organizers, the peer-to-peer rule: people respond most readily to those they regard as their peers. It makes sense. If you want to involve lawyers, it helps to have the lawyer in your core group make the approach to other lawyers. Want health professionals? Send in a health professional. Want to involve low-income parents? Ask a low-income parent in your group to do the recruiting. If your core group includes all the critical stakeholders, you should have built-in peer recruiters.

Policy makers know they need the support of 51% (of their colleagues on a Committee, the members of the House or Senate, the voters in their District) to make anything happen. When we come to them with an idea or request, they will automatically start to consider whether it is something capable of winning 51% of the relevant vote. That is why it helps if from the outset your list of coalition members suggests breadth as well as self-interest – like the Florida police who teamed up with after-school-care advocates because children in organized pro-

> "having even a few odd couples sends a political signal that you are reaching out and talking to more than others who already agree with you."

grams are less likely to get in trouble with the police (their slogan: *Cops Care for After-School Care*). The organization Fight Crime: Invest in Kids involves the same politically effective combination of child care and law enforcement on a nation scale.

## 2. SELECT A GOOD ISSUE.

Some issues are too narrow (or too localized) to warrant a coalition, and you do not want to get a reputation for calling for coalitions anytime you cannot handle a job. But anything that affects the community at large (environmental hazards, Medicaid eligibility limits, whether food is taxed, affordable housing) might be a good issue for a coalition.

## 3. CALL AN ORGANIZING MEETING TO SET A GOAL.

If you think you have got a good issue, and you want to see community groups work together to resolve it, try the idea out on some key community players and invite them to join you at a brown bag/brain-storming lunch. You will quickly discover whether there is enough interest in your issue – or whether there is something else on which you all can work together.

# The Other Side

**Despite the many benefits of working together in coalitions, some groups hesitate to join. Drawbacks include:**

- Logistics become more complicated. It is hard enough to set up a meeting with six people you know. Convening meetings of thirty organizations, some of whom you only know slightly or by reputation, is much harder.

- Getting agreement is harder, e.g., on who votes, who takes responsibility for what, and matters of style.

- Credit, as well as blame, gets shared. Your group may not get as much visibility; alternatively, if one member of the coalition behaves badly, all may be tarnished. There is also the fear (unfounded) that everyone in a coalition has to agree with everything every member says or does.

- Decision-making must be shared. Some organizations have by-laws or Board structures that make it hard to submit to group decision-making.

**Happily, there are good answers to most of the above. For example:**

- Responsibility for logistical support can rotate among groups.

- Key contact lists can identify decision-makers from key groups who can speak for their members on short notice, and can quickly disseminate information throughout their networks.

- It is possible to set up a time-limited, single-issue campaign rather than an on-going, multi-issue coalition.

- Endorsements can be structured so that member groups can opt in or out, provision-by-provision. Or participants can agree that for purposes of a particular campaign, every group on the list will promise not to work *against* any other group on the list. They do not have to work *for* what someone else wants, they just will not allow the politicians to pit one against another for now. (This device has occasionally enabled even pro-life and pro-choice groups to work together in coalitions, around the need for good maternity care, or very discrete issues.)

# Working With the Media

Whether an issue gets the attention of the politicians may depend on whether it has the attention of the media. Good advocates regard the media as deserving as much attention as working with elected officials and working with the grassroots. There are three reasons: politicians pay attention to the media (it provides a way to check the community pulse); media can be used to reach other voters; and misinformation that appears in the media needs to be challenged.

Childcare standards provide a good example of how this works. They got very little attention until some dramatic stories turned up in the media of children harmed while in unregulated care. That drew attention to the issue and also gave worried parents a forum in which to express their concerns. Legislative hearings followed, as did many more state laws requiring that childcare providers meet basic health and safety standards.

There are so many issues competing for the attention of decision-makers that good advocates need to work with the media to get action. That is not as hard as you may think.

"Good advocates regard the media as deserving as much attention as working with elected officials and working with the grassroots."

**The media Include:**

- Newspapers, magazines, newsletters (including those put out by your faith community, professional organization, or any groups you belong to);

- Television (news, features, cable access, and Public Service Announcements – PSA's);

- Radio stations (especially news, features, talk shows, and PSA's);

- Websites (your own, or the links you provide on your website to advocacy groups you trust – both can be used for position papers, fact sheets, even lengthy reports); and

- New media including Facebook, Twitter, YouTube, and blogs.

Ultimately, "the media" are just individuals, including people you know. If you watch for the names at the top of news stories and regular columns on issues you care about, and listen for the names of the producers and editors of any radio shows that might be interested, then you can ask for them by name. If you cannot get an individual's name, use a title. "Assignment editor" is one that will often get you the right person, or "Producer." You need to get your issue known and talked about as much as possible, and the media are your route to that end.

It helps to realize that the media are like most institutions: white men still hold most of the high-ranking positions, so they get the preferred, daytime hours. On the weekends, women and minorities are more likely to be in charge. If the regular assignment editor rejects your story, try again on the weekend – you may get a different response.

If you can afford to assign a staff person to work at least part-time with media, effective media work for that person will include:

- Learning how to write a press release or backgrounder.

- Making calls directly to news organizations.

- Establishing a relationship with reporters who cover your issues.

- Observing deadlines (do not call a TV station at 4:00 p.m. with an item for the 6:00 p.m. news; do not bother radio reporters just before airtime; give everybody plenty of lead time for a complicated story).

- Considering their needs (TV needs something to film; radio needs something with good sound; newspapers are more likely to use tables or charts and do interviews by phone).

- Recognizing their limitations (e.g., TV news is now primarily a headline service for stories that can be told in 60 to 75 seconds – they do not do well with complicated or subtle issues: for that you need to approach newspapers or radio).

- Being accurate (you will not get trusted as a source, or called a second time, if you feed reporters unchecked or shaky information).

- Becoming comfortable with and using various new media tools. Establishing relationships with key community or issue-specific bloggers (by directly contacting them, offering them tips, partnering with them if and where appropriate, reposting their materials on your website or blog, and sharing their posts on your Facebook and Twitter profiles) is becoming increasingly important for organizations that want to engage with the media. Also keep in mind that many traditional media reporters and editors (and their publications) are also now on Facebook, Twitter, and other social media sites, so posting regular updates, sharing news coverage of your organization, and more can grab the media's attention in a way that a traditional press release or press call may not.

**"If you don't have staff assigned to work on media, be creative."**

If you don't have staff assigned to work on media, be creative. A supporter of the arts in Illinois noticed that when his daughter became editor of her high school newspaper, she was eager for story ideas to assign her reporters. Guessing that might be the case for others as well, he invited the editors of his community's three high school newspapers over for a brainstorming conversation. Over pizza he suggested they do a five-part series on "Youth and the Arts," and he suggested ideas for some elements in the series. In particular, he suggested that they interview the state and local elected officials from their communities, to learn their positions on public fundraising for performing and visual arts. When the various series were published, he urged the editors to send copies to elected officials from their area, so they would see themselves in print on the topic. Bright young high school seniors (most of an age to vote for the first time) got engaged with their elected officials, plus elected officials knew that teachers, parents, and other school personnel were reading their replies to the students' questions. That's a great example of low-cost, creative media work.

The advocacy community itself is a good resource when it comes to working with the media. Some have publications to help members present particular issues to the media. Many put on workshops and roleplaying sessions on how to deal with the media. (See OMB Watch's 'Take Action' page at www.ombwatch.org/get_involved)

Savvy national advocacy groups try to help local advocates win media attention – as when the Food Research and Action Center sent local hunger advocates advance copies of a report on childhood hunger and worked with them to set up local press conferences pegged to the release of the national data. In that way, advocates all across the country were ready when network affiliates and local newspapers wanted a local angle on the national story, and the media coverage was better than it would have been. (State-level advocates can use the same approach with their local affiliates, to get better statewide coverage.)

### Do Not Forget

As intimidating as the idea of working with the media may seem at the outset, you are media consumers. That means you can invite someone from the local media to explain to your group how they work. Remember also that they are always looking for good stories, and you may have one.

ONE WORD OF WARNING: Never say anything to a member of the working press that you would not want to see attributed to you in the news the next day. You are always "on the record" when speaking to or e-mailing anyone in the press.

# Techniques for the Politically Shy

Across the country, community groups have been developing their own, easily adapted ways of influencing policies. Often they serve more than one end. Here are examples of techniques that can be used.

For those who are just getting started, or trying to get other advocacy novices involved, it helps if the advocacy effort has elements that are:

*❋ Easy, fun, low-cost, and able to attract the media ❋*

### FOLDERS

A Junior League member in Denver noted that when she began spending time at the City Council and State Legislature, no one had any reason to know who she was or the group she represented. But she quickly realized that whenever she went to a Council meeting or the Capitol, she always carried a folder with her fact sheets and other basic information about the issues on her group's legislative agenda. So, she made up clear, large-type labels identifying her group and/or key issue (e.g., Support Child Care – We Do), to put on her folders. Then, she just had to remember to carry her folder so the label and message were visible.

Folders with a message are something anyone can carry, including people with limited education or knowledge of English, and people too shy to speak out. This way, even an absolute newcomer who does not say a word (e.g., residents from a group home, immigrants, homeless youths) can be a visible presence, a first-time advocate.

## BADGES/T-SHIRTS

Badges can serve a similar function. That is why the real pros make them large, in bold colors, and easy to read. Badges with tiny print and a complicated message cannot be read from a distance.

"Some groups and coalitions try to have a few members at the legislature every week on the same day."

Some groups and coalitions try to have a few members at the legislature every week on the same day. They use common badges (in a bold color, with the coalition name as well as space for the member) to make the point that they are a persistent, consistent presence – even though they cannot afford to have a professional lobbyist or the same people at the Capitol every week.

A Healthy Mothers/Healthy Babies advocate in Michigan had a similar notion: on weekends and every day during summer vacation she makes a point of wearing a T-shirt with a message promoting her issue…and encourages others to. For them, just walking through the grocery store becomes an advocacy opportunity.

## EDUCATIONAL PETITIONS

Advocates for the hungry and homeless in Phoenix used an annual holiday fund drive to gather names on a petition. Every time a donation was made, the donor was asked to also sign their petition. It read something like, "We the undersigned are doing our part to meet food and shelter needs in our community. Now we are calling on our legislators at all levels to do their part and adequately fund the programs to help vulnerable people." They made the point that charity alone is not enough – in a way that educated the voting public, and sent a message to their elected officials.

## CONTESTS

Want to generate a lot of letters or postcards in favor of your issue? Stage a contest. Advocates at one children's hospital offered "Comp Days," donated NBA tickets, restaurant vouchers, and other prizes to the staff that turned in the most accurately filled-out post-cards (signed, personalized, with voters' home address). Before long the various units (nurses, ER, clerical staff, laundry, trustees…) were competing with one another. The "young docs" even set up a dunk tank in front of the hospital – with completed post cards for the campaign as the price for throwing balls to "dunk the docs."

## PHONES

Advocates in several states are using "Paper cell phones" cut from brightly colored card stock, that contain the telephone number of their state capitol (or in some cases, the names and numbers of the legislators from their district), the hours the switchboard is open, and their state legislature's web site. At gatherings of any size they pass the paper "phones" out to everyone. First they do one role-play of a call to the Capitol for all to hear, and then they ask everyone present to pair up with the person next to them to try a sample legislative "call." One plays the part of the operator, and the other plays the constituent. A volunteer can actually place a call and put it on speakerphone for all to hear. Participants take the paper "phones" home to perch on their telephones or computers, to serve as a reminder each time a legislative alert comes in.

When the pastor of one small, inner-city congregation learned about paper "phones," she quickly grasped a use for them. As she explained, many of her congregants were elderly and poor, but they had time, and they had telephones. She organized about 10 who felt willing to try making calls, and now when a legislative alert comes in, they are poised and ready: one calls at 9:15, the next at 9:30, another at 9:45…They've become well-known to their legislators' offices, and they even have a name: the *Call Girls*.

## ADVOCACY LINKED TO OTHER OPPORTUNITIES

A common way to raise money for local services is to get pledges for every mile someone walks or runs. A group in Milwaukee used one such occasion for a little lobbying. At the rest stops they had post cards, and the names and addresses of local legislators. Anyone stopping for juice or water could also write a quick note in support of the object of the run. The group in charge got the names and addresses of those who wrote cards (individuals who may be interested in taking a next step), as well as a possible media story.

A different pledge tack was taken when hate-mongers announced plans to disrupt an event featuring gay/lesbian/transgender student leaders. Supporters of the students asked people to pledge money for every minute the hate-mongers carried on – and then gave the proceeds to an advocacy group working for gay/lesbian/transgender rights. That way the award ceremony was not disrupted by a shouting match, and civil rights advocacy was supported.

# Techniques for Working With Policy Makers

When you are ready to deal directly with policy-makers, the same general rules apply. Whenever possible make it easy to do, low cost, and enjoyable for people to participate. But also:

> ✳ *Be informed. Be concise. And be clear about what you want.* ✳

Do not be embarrassed to be direct – as a citizen and advocate, your job is to *ask;* their job is to *be asked*. And do not worry – if you are asked a question to which you do not know the answer, that is no problem. Just say: "I do not know the answer to that, but I'll find out and get back to you." Then do.

## TUESDAYS ON THE HILL

A large urban Council of Churches wanted to make it easier and more comfortable for members to come and lobby their state legislators. They could not eliminate the distance or time involved (two major barriers), but they could eliminate the other reasons people stay away: feeling inexperienced, or uninformed.

They advertised through congregation bulletins that anyone who wished to lobby on social justice issues could come to the Capitol on Tuesday mornings, about two hours before most meetings were set. The time would be used to make people smart: do briefings, explain bills, provide fact sheets, and answer questions.

They also did something very reassuring: *they paired beginners who had never lobbied before with an experienced "buddy,"* someone who would spent a lot of time at the Capitol. That way first-timers did not need to say anything unless they wanted to; just being there was a learning experience and a contribution. After tagging along with a more experienced person a few times, almost anyone feels competent to lobby on their own – and even take someone else who is less experienced.

Anything can be intimidating the first time (tying your shoes was hard the first time). Letting advocacy newcomers tag along to watch the veterans has enormous value. It is something all good teachers - coaches, trainers, bosses, parents - understand: children learn by example; medical students learn by observing; old farmers show young farmers how to operate the machinery. Policy advocacy is no different. It is possible to read a book and just plunge in, but watching someone more experienced the first time or two makes learning much easier.

## LEGISLATORS AS MODERATORS OR PANELISTS

If you already know your legislators' positions, but wish they knew more about yours, there are several models to draw from.

A human services coalition in Connecticut invites key legislators to moderate panels (not as speakers), and uses the panelists for what amounts to a *seminar* for the legislator. (This is well suited to explaining some complex community issue not easily summarized in a fact sheet.)

A South Carolina group used the workshop period of their annual conference to hold mini-hearings at which their members were the witnesses, and key legislators were asked to serve as moderators. The participants got a brief - three minute - opportunity to practice giving testimony, after which the legislators gave tips on what makes for good testimony, and everyone learned from each other – including the legislators who were, in effect, being lobbied. (This same device could be used when inviting a legislator to a university class or to a group's membership meeting.)

In North Carolina, a mental health organization used the workshop sessions at their annual conference for specially constructed panels. Each panel consisted of three consumers of state services, plus two legislators and a moderator. Among the consumers was the parent of an emotionally disturbed child, a recovering alcoholic, and someone with a mental illness. The legislators learned first-hand how the laws were being implemented, and also got a glimpse of needed changes. It was another effective way to use a conference workshop session to education (and in some cases lobby) elected officials.

## ANNOUNCE A CALL-IN DAY

Often the people you would like to involve as advocates cannot get to the Capitol or a meeting with their legislators. That might apply to anyone with a limited income, young children, demanding job, physical disability, or troubled family member. But it is very important that their voices be heard, and call-in days are one way to make that possible.

Texas groups representing people with disabilities were among the first to use their newsletters and e-mail lists to announce that the day after a "Lobby Day at the Capitol" would be a "Call-In Day." Everyone was urged to make three phone calls: to the Governor, their legislator, and the Speaker of the House. A sample script was provided. That way, members of the legislature spent one day in personal visits from those who could get to the Capitol, and another day on phone calls/phone messages from those who could not visit personally. It was doubly effective without being twice as costly.

This same device is increasingly used on items before the U.S. Congress. It is hard for most people to get to Washington, D.C., and in any case there is often too little time to arrange for letters or visits. This is especially true when there is a need to call attention to some small item in a large, complex budget bill – or when votes come up with little notice. And, it is a good use for a call to members to "Take Five."

When e-mail was new (and little-used) it was common for advocacy groups to urge a mass e-mail campaign. Now that e-mail is so common it can be less effective. Governors, members of Congress, and even some state legislators, are increasingly likely to require that e-mail correspondents send their letters through a web site – one that requires a name and address in the legislator's home district – where it may not be noticed or responded to for several days. The sheer volume of e-mail can make it problematic. On the other hand, people sitting in the visitors' gallery at most state legislatures can look down and see legislators with their laptops open, reading and replying to their e-mail messages between votes.

The best advice is to always ask your legislators whether or not they like hearing from constituents by e-mail. If they say, "yes," use it; if they say, "no," use the phone or regular mail.

## USE SKYPE

When distance is an issue, ask your legislators to "meet" via Skype. One member (or your lobbyist) can be present in their office, while a group joins the meeting via Skype from back home in the district.

## SEND THANK YOU NOTES

Elected officials deserve to be thanked for policies that work and budget decisions that help make a difference. Since they most often hear from those who want to complain, they are likely to remember those who say "thank you."

A multi-service agency in Northern Wisconsin encourages the beneficiaries of one program each month to write thank-you notes to the legislators who determine their fate. In mid-winter the recipients of energy assistance write, and in summer the youth in summer jobs write. Twelve times a year the legislators learn about the consequences of their votes, as well as good reasons to support the programs again.

> But it is very important that their voices be heard, and call-in days are one way to make that possible."

A retired couple in Washington sent their state legislators a simple two-part message. Part one was brief, it read: *"Thank You. We know this is a difficult year, and we are asking you to make difficult choices. We appreciate it."* Part Two read: *"Tax us. We're for gas taxes, luxury taxes, and 'sin' taxes. If casino and other gambling taxes are on the table, include them. And yes, we think the main source of governmental funding that is not now taxed is the wealth of us at the top..."* One legislator replied: *"You cannot imagine how welcome – and rare – your letter was."*

## REWARD GOOD GOVERNMENT ACTION

If policy makers only hear from those who want less government, they will think cutting back is always the best response. Advocates can help provide another perspective.

In North Carolina, a child advocacy group gave awards to the counties doing the best job of serving eligible children. Counties with the best records in reaching the most Medicaid-eligible (WIC-eligible, child care eligible, summer lunch-eligible...) children were honored at their annual conference. Program administrators, media representatives, and local elected officials were invited to attend from the winning counties, and bring a five-minute power point or video presentation to display their winning techniques. That sent a powerful message to officials and voters alike about the value of the programs.

## COMPILE SUCCESS STORIES

"Politicians cannot afford to be identified only with losing causes,"

Politicians cannot afford to be identified only with losing causes, which is how most complicated issues appear when they are first proposed. That is why good advocates take care to compile success stories – stories of streams saved, gang members turned poet, mural projects that change lives along with urban vistas.

Success stories can be compiled about juvenile offenders or teen parents, about revitalizing neighborhoods or new immigrants, about the benefits of local theaters or urban gardens – about all those people and causes whose futures are changed by the actions of nonprofits. *Success stories carry a powerful message that "at risk" need not mean "doomed."*

Success stories can be used to great effect during lobbying visits or when making presentations in the community (for example, before the local Association of University Women or Chamber of Commerce). It is not enough to try and scare policy-makers and policy-shapers with grim statistics, they need some proof that what you are asking for works, that the resources they commit will have results. It is that "cocktail of fear and hope" that prompts action, and hope comes in the form of evidence that we can make a difference.

**MORAL:** As each example illustrates once again, advocacy is as much a frame of mind as it is a set of skills or knowledge. Advocates have a way of seeing opportunities and using them to get important issues before the policy-makers and their staff.

But working directly with legislators and policy-makers is only one part of the job to be done. Getting the attention and understanding of the voters and the media are the others. Good advocates are always seeking ways, large and small, to do all three. They use information, fear, guilt, whatever helps... along with the evidence that what they are asking for *works*.

Policy analyst Steven Kelman says that political decisions "are the collective choices of people who disagree. Behind them stands the power of government." It is up to us to shape those "collective choices" behind which our government stands.

## The 3-Legged Stool at Work

**PARENT POWER.** In the fall of 1999, The Children's Hospital (TCH) in Denver hosted a day of advocacy training for members of the community. Among the 130 or so who came that day was the parent of a child with a rare, inherited metabolic disorder (IMD), along with a staff person from the IMD clinic.

Their goal was both simple and daunting: to convince insurance companies to cover the cost of the expensive, prescribed formula that is the only possible treatment for IMDs. For years they had tried various tactics: legal action, writing to insurance companies, attempting to negotiate with individual insurers and their representatives. So far, none of it had worked.

Now they had come to an advocacy training, not sure it would help but unwilling to leave any stone unturned. As luck would have it, a Colorado state Representative joined the training on a panel of state experts. At the next break, the two IMD advocates shyly put their newly acquired training to the test: they approached the Representative and told their story. A few months later yet another parent of an IMD child joined the effort and before long, helping IMD families win insurance coverage became a TCH legislative priority for 2001.

**CAPITOL ACTIVITY.** By January, the Representative who had attended the fall event had agreed to sponsor a bill to deal with the problem. But this apparently simple bill quickly encountered serious obstacles: the Governor, many legislators, and the state's insurance companies all made clear their opposition to any insurance mandates. Plus, only about 100 people in Colorado have an IMD – so legislators wondered whether it was worth their time and effort.

**GRASSROOTS ACTIVITY.** TCH activated its Grassroots Advocacy Network – staff, trustees, patients, and patient families – in support of the bill. IMD families rallied the support of anyone they could. Soon hundreds of people were writing and calling their legislators.

**MEDIA ACTIVITY.** The hospital helped by coordinating media stories to draw attention to the issue. One story ran three weeks before the legislature convened. Ultimately, 11 stories ran in state and local newspapers; another 13 stories were broadcast on TV. Coverage ran the gamut – from feature stories to news to editorials.

Throughout, professional lobbyists and parents alike worked to win the Governor's support, meet with insurers' representatives, forge coalitions, and lobby. At every point, families with IMD children played a critical role: testifying, conducting interviews with the media, meeting with legislators, negotiating with insurers.

One key legislator was heard to say that he had never been lobbied so hard on a proposal before and "...you claim that it only affects 100 people... I just do not think it is possible for me to hear from so many people about a bill that only affects 100 people." That is the power of grassroots.

**RESULT:** Success! After months of work, the bill passed the legislature and was sent to the Governor – who had become convinced of its importance. He signed the bill at the hospital, surrounded by IMD clinic patients and their cheering families.

# PART 05

# Fringe Benefits of Policy Advocacy

New advocacy groups are springing up everywhere, and broad coalitions of existing organizations are taking on a wide range of issues important to their communities. They are educating the public and their own members, working with the media and lobbying their elected officials. And they are winning victories large and small: preventing cuts in vital programs, changing laws and budgets, influencing public agendas.

In the early years of the 21st Century, Congress renewed the Violence Against Women Act, improved the Earned Income Tax Credit for low-earning families, improved services for the mentally ill, approved expansions of protected lands, finally passed Campaign Finance Reform, and more. And all of the laws and budgets approved had something in common: none of it happened by accident; all of it happened with the help and support of advocates in communities of every size.

Lists can also be compiled for state governments nationwide. Those lists of legislative accomplishment – the displaced workers in Minnesota who won important benefits when all the experts told them it could not be done, the immigrants in California who won critically needed food stamps benefits despite an energy-strapped budget, the low-income parents in Maryland who won increased aid to the  poorest school districts, the child advocates in Kansas who saved tobacco settlement funds from an attempted raid – all are among the direct results of policy advocacy. And note: these are victories won without the ability to write big campaign checks.

But something else is happening at the same time. Groups that began with a handful of discouraged people now boast hundreds or thousands. Those who got involved speak of feeling energized, and empowered, where before they spoke of feeling burned out, and disregarded. And they radiate an excitement that is positively contagious.

It is not because these are all super-men and super-women, but because advocacy can have that effect. These are ordinary people who have seen a need and figured out some way to try and meet it. In the process they (and the groups they belong to) are being changed. Advocacy has benefits that go far beyond the achievement of immediate goals.

# Benefits to the Individuals

You can start small. If your group wants public hearings before the county decides whether (and where) to build a new nursing home, for example, that has a relatively short timeframe as well as a very clear conclusion.

Moreover, that is something which might be accomplished in a very low-key manner – by having individuals in your group make phone calls to county commissioners they know. In cases like this, your group may not get any experience mounting a large-scale letter-writing and lobbying campaign, or working with the local media, but they will learn about low-key advocacy techniques.

The obvious way to judge that effort is in relation to the goal: did you succeed in getting public hearings held before a decision was made? Did you *win the victory* you had in mind?

But another way to judge an advocacy effort is in relation to its effect on the people involved in the effort, and whether it was carried out in a way that helped you *build the movement* for change. Even a losing effort can teach valuable lessons, including:

- How to think strategically,
- How to build trust and come to joint decisions,
- Who in your group has ties to community leaders,
- The value of reaching out to other voters, and
- How to grow a network.

"It is far more empowering to be one of those that decide, than the one being decided for."

You – and everyone involved – will also have learned what it means to be active participants in a decision, not just passive objects of decisions made by somebody else. If you are concerned with human dignity, that last point is particularly important.

That is why *empowerment* is a word so often used in describing the benefits of advocacy. It is far more empowering to be one of those that decide, than the one being decided for. That is especially true for anyone who is directly affected. If your group includes families with an ill or troubled member, single parents who are feeling over-whelmed, or people living in a changing environment, being able to influence services, supports, or zoning regulations will leave them feeling less like pawns.

*Morale* is another fringe benefit of advocacy. Those who work in nonprofits often speak of being burned out, particularly when need is rising faster than donations, budgets, or volunteers.

They, not the politicians, must say "no" when the services, money, or staff have been exhausted. Seeing need day after day, while feeling powerless to help, takes a toll that can be physical as well as psychological. An advocacy effort to protect a service, save a natural resource, increase a budget, or win better policies can be a helpful antidote to burnout.

*Attacking root causes* is also a benefit of advocacy. More than most, direct service workers (paid and volunteer) understand that more shelters will not end homelessness, and more volunteers are no substitute for decent wages or a way to pay the doctor.

Understanding that and not knowing how to change it is demoralizing. So is the sense of wanting to *do something,* anything, even if it is not the answer. Both are among the reasons there is so much staff and volunteer turn-over in the helping professions and many nonprofits: it is debilitating to wage a hopeless, ineffective war.

Advocacy offers an opportunity to change that.

> "Working to fix a bad system is far more satisfying than working to patch up mistakes after-the-fact, one frantic person or cause at a time."

Think what it would mean to be able to fight underlying causes, to make things better for tens or thousands at a time, to deal with what Raul Yzaguirre, former president of the National Council of La Raza calls, "a growing poverty of the spirit." Think how much more efficient, more effective, and more energizing it would be to know you would not have to fight the same battle over and over again.

With advocacy, that can happen. Staff that were over-whelmed and under-funded get to work for changes that will make their jobs more manageable and help more people – all at the same time. Working to fix a bad system is far more satisfying than working to patch up mistakes after-the-fact, one frantic person or cause at a time.

# Benefits to the Organization

Whenever an advocacy effort is undertaken in the name of a sponsoring group, the benefits accrue to more than just the individuals involved, in the same way that a small committee may be responsible for a fundraiser but everyone in the group benefits from the money they bring in.

### IT HELPS DEVELOP TRUE CONSTITUENCIES

Sometimes a handful of vocal people become an issue's spokespeople by default. A good advocacy effort changes that.

By seeking out the views of those being spoken for, it helps develop constituencies – those affected by the issue, potential supporters and their organizations – and gives them a voice. And if the advocacy effort is managed with integrity, your organization will become more accountable to those you speak for, as well as less easily dominated by a vocal few.

nfy
onff efdoffrn

## IT HELPS BUILD ORGANIZATIONAL STRUCTURES

Nothing complex can be carried out without policies and procedures, roles and responsibilities, methods and mechanisms, all carefully spelled out and assigned. Your group will learn just by deciding on its own structure: should the Core Committee be big or small? Is the campaign short-term or long-term? The procedures formal or informal? Decisions reached by majority or consensus?

Working out those practical questions and living by the decisions builds organizations.

## IT IS A WAY TO IDENTIFY AND DEVELOP NEW LEADERSHIP

The very fact that a new effort is about to be undertaken will interest those who have taken on leadership roles in the past.

But it is also likely to attract the involvement of some who have been invisible before, and among them will be potential new leaders – old and young – with previously unrecognized talents. Developing new leadership pays off many times over, for everything your group hopes to accomplish (including attracting new members), and not just the immediate issue.

## ADVOCACY EFFORTS HELP TO EDUCATE THE PUBLIC

They provide natural opportunities to educate yourselves, your group, and others about the policy process and the unmet needs of your community.

Because advocacy efforts tend to have high public visibility, they also offer opportunities to educate the larger community about your organization's perspective on important community issues, as well as your role in dealing with them. In that sense it is a form of advertising or outreach.

People in need of services will learn what you provide, as will many who may have been unaware of your group's existence.

Advocacy efforts help establish (or improve) relations with community leaders.

To be successful, you will need to identify and become known to a variety of community leaders. You may begin by wanting those relationships to advance specific elements of your advocacy campaign, but having established relationships with elected officials and the heads of various community institutions and groups (and their staffs), you may call upon them for other purposes as well.

# Benefits to the Democratic Process

In the normal course of events, public policies are more likely to reflect immediate concerns over cost and efficiency than long-range concerns over what we all need for a better future. But it is almost impossible to devise well-rounded policies if the people most concerned about others refuse to get involved.

Think who is most likely to have a voice in the policy-making process and what their priorities are likely to be, and you will understand why you need to get involved. It is often said that, in a democracy, decisions are made by a majority of the people. Not true: decisions are made by a majority of those who get involved, and who vote.

In a participatory democracy, a policy debate reflects what the participants bring to it. So, if those who care about the broader community and not just their own narrow self-interest opt out of the process, policy-makers lose the benefit of an important perspective.

The same point applies to the perspective of nonprofits. We do not want doctors prescribing treatment without ever seeing a patient or lawyers deciding what to plead without talking to their clients. Neither should we adopt policies about public health, social services, the arts, or the environment without hearing from the people who provide and care about them. A 24-year-old staff aide working for a legislator from a wealthy suburb may not fully appreciate what life is like for a parent with a chronically ill child, low wages, and no health coverage.

"People who work in nonprofits can help be the voices of those whom the laws are most likely to affect."

People who work in nonprofits can help be the voices of those whom the laws are most likely to affect. They can be their surrogates on occasion, the eyes-and-ears of the policy process on others, and all the time they can bring valuable insights into a process that might otherwise be dictated by media interests and big campaign contributors. When those who understand first-hand refuse to become involved, the entire process is poorer for it.

# Benefits to Society

Occasionally it seems as though advocacy is just a high-stakes, fast-paced, adrenaline-pumping, hard ball game played to be won.

It is all that, and it is also much more. Public laws and budgets affect all of our lives and the lives of our communities in countless ways every day. They affect who will get help and on what terms; they help determine who lives and who dies; they determine whether natural resources will be protected or exploited. Public policies even help determine whether our communities are more divided or united.

But advocacy is not only about winning, and a sense of community does not depend solely on victories. Sometimes advocacy efforts are important to take on even when the odds seem hopelessly stacked against any possibility of success. Five are worth noting.

### 1. WHEN IT IS WHAT YOUR CONSTITUENCY WANTS

As advocates you have to use your best judgment about when to proceed and when to use your resources, but you also have an obligation to respond to your constituents. They may want something you regard as unrealistic, but one of your jobs is to convey what your constituents want and feel they need. Sometimes you may just win – like the smoking-cessation "Davids" who took on the tobacco industry "Goliath" when many thought that victory was impossible.

### 2. WHEN IT SERVES TO EDUCATE THE PUBLIC

Advocates often think in terms of two and three-year plans. Typically the first year is assumed to be for public education – with little expectation of early political action. But you cannot get political action on a non-issue. Public consciousness has to be raised; the media and public have to be educated. That cannot occur in a vacuum. Framing an advocacy issue and developing a campaign (e.g., getting a legislator to introduce a bill, or setting out three demands) will sharpen the topic and give focus to any education efforts.

## 3. TO BUILD MEMBERSHIP OR RALLY DEMORALIZED TROOPS

It is far easier to organize people for a specific goal than for a generalized, hypothetical issue. Developing an advocacy campaign can energize old members and attract new ones.

## 4. WHEN THE GROUP AFFECTED IS SOCIALLY ISOLATED

People with a mental illness or full-blown AIDS do not carry as much weight in our political system as healthy millionaires or deep-pocket trade associations, but their interests should be just as vigorously defended, just as competently represented. Advocacy can do that, while sending a powerful signal that somebody cares.

## 5. WHEN MORALITY DEMANDS IT; WHENEVER THERE IS INJUSTICE

Fighting apartheid often seemed hopeless but it was the right thing to do. If there are people in your community who are mistreated or go without care because of deeply-held prejudices (because of race or gender or income or whatever) it would be wrong *not* to do battle on their behalf, no matter how unlikely the chances of success.

In our democracy, public policies are a direct reflection of those who choose to get involved. Just as corporate farmers tend to shape agriculture policies and defense contractors influence military procurement policies, so are the policies affecting fragile environments or vulnerable people shaped by those who choose to get involved.

**Never forget:** laws and budgets will be adopted with us or without us; the choice is ours. Happily, whole communities benefit when we get involved, and they suffer when we do not. Getting involved is no guarantee of victory, but when we do win – well, there is just nothing sweeter.

Jane Addams – who helped immigrant families with everything from literacy classes and musical evenings to child care and hot baths, who served on the school board, fought for women's suffrage, and won the Nobel Prize for Peace in 1931 – understood better than most why each of us must act. She said:

*"Nothing could be worse than the fear that one has given up too soon and left one effort unexpended which might have saved the world."*

## Reality Check

Once you have identified any gaps in your advocacy system, identified the priority areas for increased advocacy capacity, and drafted a legislative agenda, ask yourself the following: Does everyone you are expecting to be advocates (including Board and staff) feel comfortable talking about your issues and the programs you care most about?

- Does your group have the expertise to carry out your advocacy plans? If not, can you get it?

- How much time will your advocacy plan require? Do you have the time?

- How much will it cost? Can you afford it?

- Will engaging in the advocacy activities have benefits beyond immediate legislative goals? (For example, will it increase community understanding? Reach out to potential new advocates? Increase diversity? Empower those affected? Build your movement?)

- Will the advocacy activity help current leadership or staff?

- Will it burden current leadership or staff?

**NOTE:** If the answer to any of these reality check questions proves worrisome, you either need to re-think your advocacy plans, or build in steps to deal with the gaps.

For example, you could arrange briefings and develop talking points for Board members or staff; you might raise funds specifically to enhance advocacy capacity; you could recruit individuals with specific talents; or you might scale back (or gradually phase in) your plans.

# Appendix

# Organizing: What Holds it All Together?

All too often advocates find it easier to assemble their statistics and spell out the arguments for their position than to organize the citizens capable of using those facts and arguments to win better policies from decision-makers. That is not a winning strategy. Facts, statistics, and research – all are important. But in a political context, even the best information in the world is no substitute for good organizing. Facts alone rarely persuade politicians; organized voters using facts in a politically savvy way often do.

Good advocates know the importance of bringing people together (i.e., organizing) to get, keep, and use power to solve problems or improve conditions for people they care about; and they know the value of organizing coalitions (i.e., an organization of organizations).

Organizing is the building block essential to making your advocacy efforts work.

(A good resource on this topic is, ORGANIZING FOR SOCIAL CHANGE: a Manual for Activists in the 1990s, by Bobo, Kendall, and Max; Seven Locks Press, 1991.)

# Are You Advocacy Ready?

Advocacy takes many forms and a good advocacy system will have elements of each. Using this list, identify the strengths and weaknesses in your community's (or your group's) advocacy system. Review it once or twice a year – check your progress. Keep in mind that advocacy is just about Speaking Up – but in ways which help our institutions work as they should. Good advocacy helps everyone enjoy the benefits, services, and/or rights to which they are entitled.

Rate each of the following forms of advocacy as it exists in your community or group as poor, ok, or excellent.

## Case Advocacy ❏ POOR ❏ OK ❏ EXCELLENT

This form of advocacy focuses on helping individuals deal with complicated systems to get the services or benefits they need. It is the first step for many. It is especially important to families with a mentally or physically disabled member. They quickly learn that speaking up is essential, but acting case-by-case is far too slow and not enough – which is when "case" turns to "cause."

## Community Education ❏ POOR ❏ OK ❏ EXCELLENT

This form of advocacy is designed to influence ordinary citizens as well as opinion-makers through information. It includes such activities as: asking a carefully-crafted question at a public forum, wearing a message T-Shirt, speaking up at the PTA or Kiwanis, carrying out a Media Campaign, and/or helping to analyze and publicize policies, statistics, and chart books.

## Capitol-Based Advocacy ❏ POOR ❏ OK ❏ EXCELLENT

This is where professional lobbyists as well as concerned citizens fit it in. Included are activities in the state Capitol during the legislative session that are intended to win better budgets and laws. It includes sending out legislative alerts, testifying, participating in lobby days, and coming to visit your legislators and their staff when personal contact from the voters is critical.

## Grassroots Advocacy ❏ POOR ❏ OK ❏ EXCELLENT

This includes everything you do from back home to influence the legislative process: writing letters, responding to legislative alerts, maintaining an effective telephone tree, expanding your network, forming coalitions of likely allies and unlikely allies, supporting good candidates, and sponsoring forums for citizens and legislators.

## Media Work ❏ POOR ❏ OK ❏ EXCELLENT

This includes developing relationships with print and electronic journalists in the community, participating in Editorial Board meetings, writing OP/ED pieces and letters-to-the-editor, as well as commenting on radio and TV coverage of your issues. Good media work involves generating positive coverage, as well as countering the negative.

# Policy Advocacy: Bite-Sized

Here are five ideas for fitting advocacy into busy lives.
They spring from one simple fact: **Advocacy Just Means Speaking Up.**

## STEP 1: SIGN UP FOR "GOOD ALERTS"

Get on a list for regular information about legislative actions likely to affect your issue/program. They will keep you informed, provide a sample "message," and help you know when your voice is needed most.

## STEP 2: USE THE TELEPHONE OR WRITE

Some states have a toll-free hotline to their State Capitol; others have a regular number. Operators will take your call, or take your message, or transfer you to your legislator's office. Whatever the method, it only takes about two minutes – because you can use the message provided in the "alert" you signed up for in Step #1.

Or you can send a simple email message. Mention the bill number or issue in the subject line, state clearly what you want the legislator to do, and be sure to put your real name and home address so they know that you live in their Legislative District. Keep it short and to the point.

Finding telephone numbers and/or email addresses is easy: just go to the website for your state Capitol, and follow directions for finding your legislators. Or, contact the League of Women Voters.

## STEP 3: HELP OTHERS TO...

• Make cardstock "telephones" with the Capitol website, telephone number, and the dates when the Legislature is in Session. Add your own logo, website, or agency name. Make up a supply, and give them to everyone you encounter: board members, staff, consumers, friends, neighbors, extended family.... You and they should pledge to make one toll-free call or email every week the legislature is in Session.

• Set up a "TAKE FIVE" table. Help others write or call their elected officials in 5 minutes or less. Bring a laptop and/or cell phone and use the handout headed "Take Five." Or use it to sign people up for your Network, or send messages about a budget item or issue.

## STEP 4: ADVERTISE YOUR ISSUE, NOT PRODUCTS

• Anytime you are around elected officials (e.g., at a City or County Council hearing, a Town Hall Meeting, at the state Capitol, etc.), wear or carry something (a conspicuous badge, a briefcase, or bag) that identifies you with your issue or agency. Bold lettering on a neon background will be seen even from a distance – e.g., FEED KIDS, or, SUPPORT the PTA.

The politicians present will quickly realize those badges mean there's an organized group that cares about a particular issue, and has its members in the audience.

• Write a slogan or the name of your group on the folder holding your "fact sheets" or handouts. Then carry the folder to Hearings or Candidate Forums so the slogan shows.

## STEP 5: MENTION KEY BILLS, ISSUES, AND BUDGET ITEMS AT EVERY OPPORTUNITY

Talk to anybody who will listen: at a PTA meeting, in a grocery store line, waiting for the street light to change, after services on Sunday.... Get your key issues on other voters' radar screens.

**USEFUL TIP:**

It helps if you prepare a "60-Second Speech," ready for any occasion when you might get to talk to an elected official or decision-maker. For example, you might run into your state Senator at the local farmers' market or you might spot the aide to a County Council member where you worship. Those are great opportunities for a quick bit of advocacy.

Here are two versions for what to include:

# SPEECH A

❏ Your name, and where you live (Hi, I'm _____, and I live in your District.)

❏ Your group or agency – mention the number of members or people served in the elected's District (I'm on the board of DAWN – Domestic Abuse Women's Network; we're located in your District and we serve about 300 women every month...)

❏ Say what you want to call to their attention. (I'm very concerned about adequate funding for domestic violence programs...)

❏ Say what you'd like them to do (Please vote for DV funding in the budget...)

❏ Give them something in writing that includes how to contact you/your group. (I'd be glad to answer any questions you might have; meanwhile, here's some basic information about what we do...) Have a basic Fact Sheet or brochure about your program with you at all times.

# SPEECH B (include one or two of these)

❏ Your name and where you live; your group or agency (same as above);

❏ Put a human face on your program, paint a brief "word picture" – it can be about someone your group or program has helped, or about your own situation;

❏ Mention something you are doing now, that *works*;

❏ Note how your efforts help in their community, how your efforts help put public dollars to work there;

❏ Remind them: volunteers, the non-profit sector, cannot do the job alone. We can't have a "public-private partnership" if the public "partner" opts out.

# 6 Reasons for Trying When Your Elected Officials Seem "Hopeless"

Here's a familiar line: "My representatives won't listen to me no matter what I say. They believe the opposite of everything I believe. I'd be wasting my time talking to them."

*Familiar yes, but wrong!* While it is true that successful political movements work with traditional allies and "swing votes" in the political middle, good advocacy is about winning over (or neutralizing) the opposition. Here are 6 reasons for approaching elected officials who oppose your view.

---

### 1) Conveying your position is basic to good advocacy.

As citizens and voters, our job is to ask them to vote a particular way (and explain our reasons why); their job is to be asked. They can't represent you (your issue, your group) unless you tell them how you wish to be represented. That's basic.

### 2) Good advocacy shows that opposition is based on more than emotion.

It is easy to dismiss someone who has never spelled out their position as a "bleeding heart" or "all emotion, no brain." A well-articulated position is harder to ignore. Besides, making your case to elected officials is good practice, because they often reflect the views of their voters – people you also have to win over.

### 3) They and their colleagues respect constituent pressure.

If and when you *do* win your legislators over to your side, they'll need to be able to say their constituents pressed them to do it.

### 4) Even with opponents, good advocacy is a way to educate and build relationships.

Legislators take positions in part based on what they believe their constituents want and value. Your letters, telephone calls, and visits inform your elected representatives about your issues, while also conveying that there is strong support for your position. Never give any elected official the right to say, "I never heard anyone support xxxx; I'm just reflecting what my constituents want."

### 5) People and minds change.

Even the most apparently immovable legislators have been known to change their position on issues – particularly when the voters back home make clear they want a change. Twenty-five years ago almost nobody in public office was pro-environment, pro-diversity, or anti-tobacco; today, a strong number of elected officials are. They didn't change by accident, and didn't change overnight: the persistent work of good advocates was key.

### 6) Never give up.

We have to be a presence. Elected officials should *not* be allowed to case votes affecting children, families, or any vulnerable people without ever having to face them or their advocates. They need to know that someone is watching… and that someone is us.

# When Your Elected Officials Agree With You

Here's a familiar line: "My representatives are already on my side. I'd just be wasting my time and theirs talking to them." Familiar yes, but wrong.

While it is true that successful political movements build new allies and neutralize opponents, all good advocacy efforts also include ways to work with the legislators who agree with you. Don't ignore your supporters because...

## Your advocacy gives supporters a basis for their position.

Legislators take positions on issues based on their perception of what their constituents value. The more letters, telephone calls, and visits your elected representatives receive, the more you both can claim widespread support for your cause. This will help both of you in efforts to recruit other supporters and to diffuse any opposition.

## Their colleagues respect constituent pressure.

It strengthens an elected official's hand when they can tell a colleague: "I support this and I am getting mounds of mail and telephone messages from my voters. They really want me to support it."

## Advocacy is a chance to educate and build a relationship.

A supportive legislator is usually more than willing to learn more about an issue they care about. Legislators juggle lots of subjects and may be very supportive of an issue about which they have little knowledge. You can help make them better advocates by arming them with your best arguments. This is your chance to be a resource to your legislator and build a solid relationship. A good relationship may help you in the future.

## There is always more to do.

Good advocacy efforts do not stop when you hear that your representative supports your cause. Supportive legislators can add value to your efforts by talking to other legislators, publicizing your cause in their district newsletter, writing an editorial piece, giving you advice on approaching others, speaking on the floor of the legislature or in caucus, and by doing countless other tasks to help you win your issue.

## Saying thank you is part of good advocacy.

Thanking your supporters is an essential part of any political movement. Thanking legislators lets them know that you paid attention to their actions and appreciated their work. Even if you don't win, it is important to say thank you.

## People and minds change.

Even the most principled politicians have been known to change their position on issues. As time passes, a politician's values can change or advocacy from opponents can take its toll. Also, there is often pressure on politicians to compromise on controversial issues. Don't let your inaction give your supportive legislators a reason to change their minds!

# Hosting Site Visits With Your Legislators

*Site Visits* – whether at your agency or at one of your projects – are a great way to inform legislators about the work you do and the people you serve. They offer a first-hand view of what government investments and non-profits are doing for the community. Plus, Site Visits help put a human face on complex issues and budget requests. When your issue comes before them next year, you want them to have a vivid, first-hand image – something a good Site Visit will provide.

But Site Visits only work when there is good planning and preparation. Four elements are key:

## 1) The Message

What is your key message? What do you *most* want to get across to your visitors?
Given that key message, what one *image* do you most want legislators to take away about:
The work your program does? The people you work with and serve? What images (happy children, poor work space, desperate families…) do you want them to carry away?

## 2) The Setting

Given the message you want to convey, what locations/circumstances would be best?
(Think about time of day, location, area of site, what you pass to get from place to place…)

## 3) The Messengers

Who can best make your points? What programs, classes, or activities should they highlight? Who would you want present: Board members? Volunteers? Staff? Clients? Neighbors of the project? People familiar with your funding? What would you want each participant to say/do?

## 4) The Supplemental Materials

What written materials should your legislator carry away from the visit? (Think of this as an opportunity to continue your message days or weeks later.) What provides an effective reminder? What fills the Information Gaps? Are there any charts/graphs/photos, etc that may take time to digest but which provide helpful information?

## MEETING WITH YOUR ELECTED OFFICIALS

*Personal visits* are a highly effective way to help legislators understand your position or program (in surveys, legislators always cite visits as the most effective way to communicate). Legislators welcome visits from constituents. *They want you involved!* However, these are busy people, so time is critical; plan ahead and use the time well.

If you don't know who your legislators are, find the District number on your Voter Registration Card, call the local League of Women Voters or your County Clerk, or go to your state website.

If you make an appointment when the legislature/Congress is in session, remember that there is no guarantee the legislators will be able to keep it. Legislative schedules change at a moment's notice. Don't take this personally, it is just "how it is." Meeting with staff is also a good thing. In all of your visits, expect to be brief, specific, and polite.

### HERE ARE SOME TIPS FOR AN EFFECTIVE MEETING:

- Make it easy for your legislator to meet with you: offer several possibilities and do your best to accommodate them.

- Make an appointment in advance – expect to get 10-15 minutes. You can call the state Capitol for your state legislator's number; members of Congress are listed in the blue-edged pages of the telephone book, and all have websites.

- Be on time; be prepared; be polite; and be brief.

- Dress appropriately for an appointment in the legislature (not fancy, but not as you would for jogging, going to the store, or working in the yard).

- If possible, learn in advance where your legislator stands on the issue. If they are supportive, thank them.

- Don't be surprised if they don't know your program or issue – it's your job to explain it.

- Be prepared to explain how the bill (the budget item, or issue) will affect you and other voters *in the legislators' district.*

- Memorize a 60-second speech to use at the beginning of your meeting. It should include:
  - Who *you* are, and the name of any *group or Coalition* you belong to
  - The *topic* you came to talk about (e.g., the name and/or number of a bill)
  - What *action* you want them to take (e.g., we want you to vote *for*...)
  - Hand them a *Fact Sheet* with basic information about your issue or group. (This way, if the appointment is interrupted, you'll still have gotten your point across; if the appointment continues, you can elaborate. Explain how people in the District will be affected; paint a brief "word picture" of real people who are/will be affected.)

- If you don't know the answer to a question, don't panic. Say: "I don't know the answer to that, but I'll find out and get back to you..." – and then *do.*

- Before leaving, ask how *you* can be of help to *them* (more information? talking with others?).

- Follow up with a thank you note and any information that was requested.

# What it Takes to Win

Mark Twain once said: *"When you need a friend, it's too late to make one."*

That's especially true when it comes to the "friends" we need in the state legislature and among any elected officials making important decisions that affect our lives. So the question we need to answer is: How many "friends?"

And the answer is found in…

## CAPITOL MATH

| US CONGRESS | | WASHINGTON STATE | |
|---|---|---|---|
| 51 | 51% of the U.S. Senate | 25 | 51% of the State Senate |
| 218 | 51% of the U.S. House of Rep's | 50 | 51% of the State House of Rep's |
| 1 | President of the U.S. | 1 | Governor |
| 1 | You and me | 1 | You and me |

Capitol Math is simply: what it takes to win. That starts with 51% of the number in the body making the decision:

## ❏ 51% of the Senate,  51% of the House of Representatives

(You can calculate the "Capitol Math" for your state. And you should calculate the Capitol math for the legislative Committee/Subcommittee that will hear your bill. Similarly, … calculate the Capitol Math for the city/county Council where you live, if your issue is a local one.) Plus…

## ❏ The President, or Governor

(or Mayor or County Executive – the person who can "sign" or "veto"), plus…

## ❏ You and me

Because *we* can influence all of the above.

# Key Advocacy Infrastructure Resources

## Alliance for Justice: For Nonprofits and Foundations
(www.afj.org/for-nonprofits-foundations)

Information on trainings on nonprofit advocacy laws and publications, alerts on recent events impacting advocacy.

## Center on Lobbying in the Public Interest (www.clpi.org)

This training and technical assistance group offers information on effective lobbying techniques and laws governing lobbying by 501(c)(3) organizations on its site. You can also send in a message with your lobbying questions.

## Council on Foundations (www.cof.org)

Information on philanthropy, funders and policy issues that affect them.

## Independent Sector (www.independentsector.org)

IS is a national membership organization of diverse nonprofits. Their website has information on the nonprofit sector, including research and policy issues.

## National Council of Nonprofit Associations (www.ncna.org)

National network of 37 state and regional associations of nonprofits representing more than 21,000 nonprofits throughout the country.

## National Committee for Responsive Philanthropy (www.ncrp.org)

Publications and policy information on making philanthropy more responsive to the people with the least wealth and opportunity.

## OMB Watch (www.ombwatch.org)

Information on federal developments impacting nonprofit advocacy, regulation of industries, the federal budget, government accountability and availability of government information.

# Helpful Websites for Making a Difference

The following is a small sample of the increasing number of online advocacy vehicles and resources for individuals and organizations to make a difference at the neighborhood, community, city, state, regional, national, and international level. We are actively seeking to expand this list online, in an effort to locate and highlight complementary resources (See www.ombwatch.org). We encourage you to submit suggestions, updates, and corrections to ombwatch@ombwatch.org.

## Advocacy Project
(www.advocacynet.org)
Nonprofit virtual partnership assisting advocates who are working on the front lines for social justice, peace and human rights, through content development and dissemination, needs assessment and technical support, web site design, networking, policy analysis, and campaigning support.

## COMM-ORG: The On-Line Conference On Community Organizing and Development
(http://comm-org.wisc.edu)
Discussion list and online archive connecting the community organizing and academic worlds. Includes discussion around assessing and evaluating organizing techniques and strategies, papers and course syllabi.

## E-thepeople
(www.e-thepeople.org)
Integrates a petitioning application with Quorum's discussion methodology, allowing individuals to electronically communicate with federal, state, and local officials, and to interact with other citizens through online forums, debates, and petitions. It also provides news and updates on legislation of general interest.

## eBase
(www.ebase.org)
Free Windows-based contact management database of members, donors, volunteers, activists, funders developed by Tech Rocks.

## Groundwire
(http://groundwire.org)
Nonprofit advocacy technology training and assistance group, supporting environmental groups in the Pacific Northwest, and providing free advocacy and technology capacity assessment resources online.

## Idealist
(www.idealist.org)
A global online network of nearly 30,000 community and nonprofit organizations in over 150 countries working to create and sustain practical solutions to social and environmental problems. Idealist connects individuals and social change actors through a searchable online database and customizable e-mail notifications of events, volunteer and job opportunities, and resources.

## Internal Revenue Service

(www.irs.gov/charities)
The IRS has created a special section on its website that has information on lobbying and election rules for nonprofits, as well as publications, forms and information on reporting, tax exemption and other issues of interest.

## Midwest Academy

(www.midwestacademy.com)
Information on direct action organizing training and publications, along with online tutorials.

## National Council of State Legislatures

(www.ncsl.org)
State by state information on registration and reporting laws for lobbying.

## NPAction

(www.npaction.org)
This one-stop resource for nonprofits has a wealth of material on advocacy, including tips sheets, downloadable forms and handouts, articles explaining laws on advocacy for nonprofits, forums for sharing ideas and more. Contains tools for engaging in advocacy and links to key web sites provide vital information about strategies for success and laws governing nonprofit policy involvement. An online contact system gives visitors access to the federal government, state and local elected officials and the media. The site is sponsored by OMB Watch.

## One World

(www.oneworld.net)
An international network of over 1000 organizations organized into regional and topical online centers collaboratively hosting a directory of progressive nonprofit organizations, news, calendars, specialized policy news and reference information "mini portals" focused on specific issue areas, as well as the means to work or volunteer with organizations and engage in online advocacy campaigns.

## SPIN Project

(www.spinproject.org)
Media technical assistance to nonprofit public-interest organizations, including online tutorials on everything from developing a media plan to photo ops and media events.

## Voices for America's Children

(www.voices.org)
Information to help build the capacity of state and local child advocacy organizations containing information ranging from the basics of child advocacy to process and selection of issues.

## Virginia Organizing Project

(www.virginia-organizing.org)
This statewide grassroots organization has an Organizing Toolbox on its web site with articles and tip sheets on everything from "Build Public Relationships With Elected Officials" to "Tips For Chairing Meetings."

## VolunteerMatch

(www.volunteermatch.org)
Nonprofit online service connecting individuals with causes in their communities through a ZIP code locator service.

JUN 2 6 2000

Charity Lobbying in the Public Interest, a Project of
Independent Sector
2040 S Street, NW
Washington, DC 20009

Dear Sir or Madam:

This is in response to a letter, dated April 18, 2000, submitted on your behalf by your attorneys, in which you request information on questions related to lobbying by publicly supported charitable organizations recognized as exempt from federal income tax because they are described in section 501(c)(3) of the Internal Revenue Code. Your questions and our responses are set forth below.

1.      Is lobbying by section 501(c)(3) organizations permissible under federal tax laws?

Yes (except for private foundations under most circumstances).

2.      How much lobbying may a "public charity" (a section 501(c)(3) organization other than a private foundation or an organization testing for public safety) conduct?

There are two sets of rules, and with the exception of churches, public charities can choose which set to follow. One rule is that no substantial part of the organization's activities can be lobbying. The alternative rule, that an organization must affirmatively elect, provides for sliding scales (up to $1,000,000 on total lobbying and up to $250,000 on grass roots lobbying) that can be spent on lobbying. (The scales are based on a percentage of the organization's exempt purpose expenditures.)

3.      What are the advantages and disadvantages of the two options?

Organizations covered by the "no substantial part" rule are not subject to any specific dollar-base limitation. However, few definitions exist under this standard as to what activities constitute lobbying, and difficult-to-value factors, such as volunteer time, are involved.

Organizations seeking clear and more definite rules covering this area may wish to avail themselves of the election. By electing the optional sliding scale, an organization can take advantage of specific, narrow definitions of lobbying and clear dollar-based safe harbors that generally permit significantly more lobbying than the "no substantial part" rule. However, as noted above, there are ceilings (unadjusted for inflation) on the amount of funds that can be spent on lobbying. Thus, these dollar limits should be considered when making the election.

4.      How does a public charity elect?  May an election be revoked?

The organization files a simple, one-page Form 5768 with the Internal Revenue Service. The election only needs to be made once.  It can be revoked by filing a second Form 5768, noting the revocation.

5.      Does making the election expose the organization to an increased risk of an audit?

No.  The Internal Revenue Manual specifically informs our examination personnel that making the election will not be a basis for initiating an examination.

6.      Does the Internal Revenue Code allow public charities that receive federal grant funds and contracts to lobby with their private funds?

Yes.  However, while it is not a matter of federal tax law, it should be noted that charities should be careful not to use federal grant funds for lobbying except where authorized to do so.

7.      May private foundations make grants to public charities that lobby?

Yes, so long as the grants are not earmarked for lobbying and are either (1) general purpose grants, or (2) specific project grants that meet the requirements of section 53.4945-2(a)(6) of the Foundation Excise Tax Regulations.

8.      May section 501(c)(3) organizations educate voters during a political campaign?

Yes.  However, organizations should be careful that their voter education efforts do not constitute support or opposition to any candidate.

9.      May public charities continue to lobby incumbent legislators even though the legislators are running for reelection?

Yes.  Charities should be careful, however, to avoid any reference to the reelection campaign in their lobbying efforts.

If you have any further questions, please feel free to contact me at (202) 283-9472, or John F. Reilly, Identification Number 50-05984, of my office at (202) 283-8971.

Sincerely,

Thomas J. Miller
Manager, Exempt Organizations Technical

cc:    Mr. Thomas A. Troyer
       Caplin & Drysdale, Chartered
       1 Thomas Cir., N.W.,
       Washington, D.C. 20005

cc:    Mr. Marcus S. Owens
       Caplin & Drysdale, Chartered
       2005 Thomas Cir., N.W.
       Washington, D.C. 20005

# STATEMENT BY THE EXEMPT ORGANIZATIONS COMMITTEE
## OF THE SECTION OF TAXATION OF THE AMERICAN BAR ASSOCIATION

### PARTICIPATION BY PUBLIC CHARITIES IN THE PUBLIC POLICY PROCESS

**G**iven persistent misunderstanding within the charitable sector about the scope of permitted participation by public charities[1] in the public policy process, the purpose of this statement is to clarify the relevant federal tax rules.

Section 501(c)(3) and its predecessors have long included a statement that charities may not attempt to influence legislation as a "substantial part" of their activities. The absence of clear definitions of both "influencing legislation" and "substantial" had a predictable and powerful chilling effect on public charities' participation in the legislative process.

To dispel this chilling effect, Congress in 1976 enacted sections 501(h) and 4911 of the Code to clarify both key aspects of the rules. Section 4911 provides a detailed, and quite favorable, definition of what does — and does not — constitute lobbying. Section 501(h) establishes, as an alternative to the vague "substantial" test, specific rules on the portion of its budget a public charity can spend on lobbying activities. Both aspects of these rules were helpfully clarified

by detailed regulations issued in 1990. Under these rules, broad categories of public policy activity directly related to the legislative process are specifically excluded from the definition of lobbying.

At charities' request, Congress made the section 501(h)/4911 rules elective. Public charities (other than churches) may opt into the

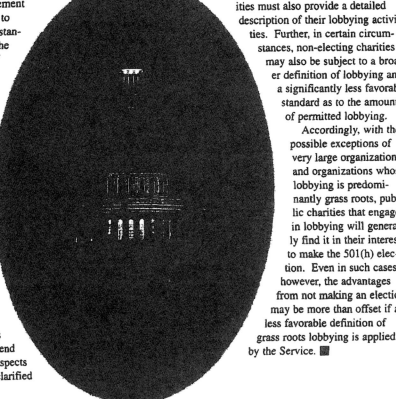

501(h)/4911 rules by filing IRS Form 5768 (a very simple, one-page form). The election is retroactive to the beginning of the tax year in which it is filed, continues in place for subsequent years, but can be revoked by the charity as to future years.

IRS officials have repeatedly stated that making the election does not increase a charity's audit risk. Nor does it increase a charity's reporting burden; indeed, electing charities are required to report only their lobbying expenditures while non-electing charities must also provide a detailed description of their lobbying activities. Further, in certain circumstances, non-electing charities may also be subject to a broader definition of lobbying and a significantly less favorable standard as to the amount of permitted lobbying.

Accordingly, with the possible exceptions of very large organizations and organizations whose lobbying is predominantly grass roots, public charities that engage in lobbying will generally find it in their interest to make the 501(h) election. Even in such cases, however, the advantages from not making an election may be more than offset if a less favorable definition of grass roots lobbying is applied by the Service. ∎

---

1.  "Public charities" are organizations exempt under section 501(c)(3) of the Internal Revenue Code which are not classified as private foundations under section 509.

# Why Your Charity Should Elect to Come Under the 1976 Lobby Law – And How to Do it

By Center for Lobbying in the Public Interest (www.clpi.org)

The right of citizens to petition their government is basic to our democratic way of life, and charitable organizations are one of the most effective vehicles for making use of citizen participation in shaping public policy. Fortunately, legislation passed by Congress in 1976 makes it possible for charities to lobby freely for their causes, communities and individuals they serve. The federal government clearly supports lobbying by charities. Congress sent this unambiguous message when it enacted the exceedingly helpful 1976 lobby law. The same message came from the IRS in regulations issued in 1990. Together, the law and regulations provide wide latitude for charities to lobby.

But the law only provides this latitude for charities that elect to be covered by it. In most circumstances, charities should become subject to this law not only because it provides liberal limits on how much they can spend on lobbying, but also because it provides very clear and helpful definitions of what activities related to legislation do not constitute lobbying. If you are formally asked to testify before a congressional committee, for example, your testimony would not constitute a lobbying expense.

Generally, organizations that elect the 1976 lobby law may spend 20% of the first $500,000 of their annual expenditures on lobbying ($100,000), 15% of the next $500,000, and so on, up to $1 million dollars!

If you do lobbying but don't elect to be subject to the 1976 law, your lobbying must be "insubstantial." This is a vague term that has never been defined. If you remain subject to this rule, you cannot be certain how much lobbying your charity can do.

Some charities have been reluctant to elect the 1976 law for fear that this action will either change their section 501(c)(3) status or serve as a "red flag" to the IRS and prompt an audit of the organization. Neither concern is justified. Electing to come under the 1976 law does not affect a charity's tax exempt status. Electing charities remain exempt under section 501(c)(3) of the Internal Revenue Code.

Further, the IRS has made clear in a letter to INDEPENDENT SECTOR that far from singling out for audit charities that elect, the reverse is true. The letter states, "…our intent has been, and continues to be, one of encouragement [of charities] to make the election… Experience also suggests that organizations that have made the election are usually in compliance with the restrictions on lobbying activities."

**Charity Lobbying. It's The Right Thing To Do!**

# The 1976 Law Governing Charity Lobbying

By Center for Lobbying in the Public Interest (www.clpi.org)

The federal government, including Congress and the Internal Revenue Service, supports lobbying by charities. Congress sent that unambiguous message when it enacted the liberal provisions under the 1976 lobby law. The same message came from the Internal Revenue Service in regulations issued in 1990, which support both the spirit and intent of the 1976 legislation.

The 1976 law is clear regarding what constitutes lobbying by charities. Following are key points about that legislation. They apply only to charities that have "elected" to come under the 1976 law.* Non-electing charities remain subject to the ambiguous "insubstantial" test. Under this test, it is unclear which charity legislation-related activities constitute lobbying and how much lobbying is permitted.

---

- The most important feature of the law is that it provides ample leeway for charities to lobby, and it protects those that elect the advantages of the 1976 rules from the uncertainties they would be subject to if they remained under the insubstantial test.

- Generally, organizations that elect the 1976 lobby law may spend 20% of the first $500,000 of their annual expenditures on lobbying ($100,000), 15% of the next $500,000, and so on, up to $1 million dollars a year! (See attached chart.) Equally important, there are eight critically important legislation-related activities that charities may conduct that are not considered lobbying by the IRS. (See "Important Lobbying Exclusions Under the 1916 Law.")

- Understanding what constitutes lobbying under the 1976 law is not difficult. In general. you are lobbying when you state your position on specific legislation to legislators or other government employees who participate in the formulation of legislation, or urge your members to do so (direct lobbying). In addition, you are lobbying when you state your position on legislation to the general public and ask the general public to contact legislators or other government employees who participate in the formulation of legislation (grassroots lobbying).

- The Internal Revenue Service encourages groups to elect to come under the 1976 law. The IRS has found groups that have elected are more often in compliance with the law than those that have not. Also it is easy to elect. Just have your governing body vote to come under the provisions of the 1976 law and file the one page IRS Form 5768 with the IRS.

\* Please see  www.clpi.org for a more detailed explanation of the 1976 lobby law.

# Lobbying Ceilings Under the 1976 Lobby Law

| Annual Exempt-Purpose Expenditures | Total Direct Lobbying Expenditures Allowable | Total Grassroots Lobbying Expenditures Allowable |
|---|---|---|
| Up to $500,000 | 20% of exempt-purpose expenditures up to $100,000 | One-quarter of the total direct lobbying expenditure ceiling |
| $500,000–$1 million | $100,000 + 15% of excess over $500,000 | $25,000 + 3.75% of excess over $500,000 |
| $1 million–$1.5 million | $175,000 + 10% of excess over $1 million | $43,750 + 2.5% of excess over $1 million |
| $1.5 million–$17 million | $225,000 + 5% of excess over $1.5 million | $56,250 + 1.25% of excess over $1.5 million |
| Over $17 million | $1 million | $250,000 |

# Form 5768

(Rev. December 1996)

Department of the Treasury
Internal Revenue Service

## Election/Revocation of Election by an Eligible Section 501(c)(3) Organization To Make Expenditures To Influence Legislation

### (Under Section 501(h) of the Internal Revenue Code)

For IRS
Use Only ▶

| Name of organization | Employer identification number |
|---|---|

| Number and street (or P.O. box no., if mail is not delivered to street address) | Room/suite |
|---|---|

| City, town or post office, and state | ZIP + 4 |
|---|---|

**1 Election**—As an eligible organization, we hereby elect to have the provisions of section 501(h) of the Code, relating to expenditures to influence legislation, apply to our tax year ending ........................................ and all subsequent tax years until revoked.

(Month, day, and year)

**Note:** *This election must be signed and postmarked within the first taxable year to which it applies.*

**2 Revocation**—As an eligible organization, we hereby revoke our election to have the provisions of section 501(h) of the Code, relating to expenditures to influence legislation, apply to our tax year ending ........................................

(Month, day, and year)

**Note:** *This revocation must be signed and postmarked before the first day of the tax year to which it applies.*

Under penalties of perjury, I declare that I am authorized to make this (check applicable box) ▶ ☐ election   ☐ revocation
on behalf of the above named organization.

| (Signature of officer or trustee) | (Type or print name and title) | (Date) |
|---|---|---|

## General Instructions

*Section references are to the Internal Revenue Code.*

Section 501(c)(3) states that an organization exempt under that section will lose its tax-exempt status and its qualification to receive deductible charitable contributions if a substantial part of its activities are carried on to influence legislation. Section 501(h), however, permits certain eligible 501(c)(3) organizations to elect to make limited expenditures to influence legislation. An organization making the election will, however, be subject to an excise tax under section 4911 if it spends more than the amounts permitted by that section. Also, the organization may lose its exempt status if its lobbying expenditures exceed the permitted amounts by more than 50% over a 4-year period. For any tax year in which an election under section 501(h) is in effect, an electing organization must report the actual and permitted amounts of its lobbying expenditures and grass roots expenditures (as defined in section 4911(c)) on its annual return required under section 6033. See Schedule A (Form 990). Each electing member of an affiliated group must report these amounts for both itself and the affiliated group as a whole.

To make or revoke the election, enter the ending date of the tax year to which the election or revocation applies in item **1** or **2**, as applicable, and sign and date the form in the spaces provided.

**Eligible Organizations.**—A section 501(c)(3) organization is permitted to make the election if it is not a disqualified organization (see below) and is described in:

1. Section 170(b)(1)(A)(ii) (relating to educational institutions),
2. Section 170(b)(1)(A)(iii) (relating to hospitals and medical research organizations),
3. Section 170(b)(1)(A)(iv) (relating to organizations supporting government schools),
4. Section 170(b)(1)(A)(vi) (relating to organizations publicly supported by charitable contributions),
5. Section 509(a)(2) (relating to organizations publicly supported by admissions, sales, etc.), or
6. Section 509(a)(3) (relating to organizations supporting certain types of public charities other than those section 509(a)(3) organizations that support section 501(c)(4), (5), or (6) organizations).

**Disqualified Organizations.**—The following types of organizations are not permitted to make the election:

a. Section 170(b)(1)(A)(i) organizations (relating to churches),

b. An integrated auxiliary of a church or of a convention or association of churches, or

c. A member of an affiliated group of organizations if one or more members of such group is described in **a** or **b** of this paragraph.

**Affiliated Organizations.**—Organizations are members of an affiliated group of organizations only if **(1)** the governing instrument of one such organization requires it to be bound by the decisions of the other organization on legislative issues, or **(2)** the governing board of one such organization includes persons (i) who are specifically designated representatives of another such organization or are members of the governing board, officers, or paid executive staff members of such other organization, and (ii) who, by aggregating their votes, have sufficient voting power to cause or prevent action on legislative issues by the first such organization.

For more details, see section 4911 and section 501(h).

**Note:** *A private foundation (including a private operating foundation) is not an eligible organization.*

**Where To File.**—Mail Form 5768 to the Internal Revenue Service Center, Ogden, UT 84201-0027.

# Four Important Facts About Lobbying With Foundation Grant Funds

By Center for Lobbying in the Public Interest (www.clpi.org)

Did you know that:

■ Public charities may use private foundation general purpose grant funds for lobbying?

■ A private foundation may make a grant to a public charity to support a project that includes lobbying as long as its own grant is less than the amount budgeted for the non-lobbying part of the project and the grant is not earmarked for lobbying?

■ Community foundations may make grants to public charities that are earmarked for lobbying?

■ Foundations may fund a number of activities that are not considered lobbying under the 1976 lobby law but affect public policy.

In short. there is considerably more latitude to use foundation funds to lobby than is commonly understood by many foundations and public charities. Following is more information.

---

**1. Using private foundation general purpose grant funds for lobbying.** Charities are not disqualified from lobbying because they receive foundation funds, but charities and, even more, foundations have been slow to recognize and act on this fact. While grant funds from a private foundation to a charity must not be earmarked for lobbying, it is perfectly legal for the charity to use unearmarked general support foundation funds to lobby. Foundation funds are considered to be earmarked only if there has been an oral or written agreement that the grant will be used for specific purposes.

**2. Using private foundation funds for the nonlobbying portion of a specific project.** A private foundation may make an unearmarked grant to support a specific project that includes lobbying, as long as its own grant is less than the amount budgeted for the nonlobbying parts of the project and the grant is not earmarked for lobbying. For example, if a specific project has a $200,000 budget, of which $20,000 is to be spent on lobbying, the private foundation can give the project up to $180,000 because that part of the project budget is allocated to nonlobbying uses.

**3. Receiving community foundation funds that are earmarked for lobbying.** Community foundations are tax exempt under section 501(c)(3) of the Internal Revenue Code and are not treated as private foundations so they are permitted the same lobbying latitude as public charities. For example, a community foundation that has elected to come under the 1976 lobby law may spend part of their annual expenditures on lobbying. It may also grant earmarked funds to a charity for lobbying up to the limits permitted by law. A community foundation grant, earmarked for lobbying, would count against the community foundation's own lobbying ceiling.

**4. Foundation funding of activities that are not lobbying but are related to public policy.** There are eight public policy related activities that charities may conduct which are not considered lobbying under the 1976 lobby law and therefore can be fully funded by foundations. For example, a charity's response to written requests from a legislative body (not just a single legislator) for technical advice on pending legislation is not considered lobbying.

The foregoing information is for general guidance and is not intended to replace legal counsel. Additional information is available from the Center for Lobbying in the Public Interest website at www.clpi.org or Center for Lobbying in the Public Interest, 2040 S Street, NW, Washington, DC 20009, Telephone: (202) 387-5048.

# Restrictions on Use of Federal Funds for Lobbying

By OMB Watch (www.ombwatch.org)

### Q: WHO IS SUBJECT TO RESTRICTIONS ON USE OF FEDERAL FUNDS FOR LOBBYING?

**A:** Nonprofits that get federal funds through categorical grants, contracts or cooperative agreements, whether directly or through an intermediary. Hospitals, universities, state and local government agencies, public nonprofits like the Legal Services Corporation and large nonprofits are governed by separate OMB rules.

### Q: WHAT ACTIVITY CANNOT BE PAID FOR WITH FEDERAL FUNDS?

**A:** "Disallowed" costs that cannot be reimbursed include:

- Attempts to influence legislation in Congress or state legislatures by direct contact with legislators
- Grassroots appeals that have a "reasonably foreseeable consequence of leading to concerted action"
- Legislative liaison work, including attending hearings, tracking and analyzing bills
- Gathering and publicizing information about actions of elected officials
- Research and nonpartisan analysis made in knowing preparation for lobbying
- Referendum campaigns
- "Electioneering," including helping candidates, parties or PACs
- Lobbying for awarding or renewal of a grant, contact or cooperative agreement

### Q: WHAT ARE THE EXCEPTIONS TO THESE PROHIBITIONS?

**A:** Exceptions allow lobbying in the following circumstances:

- Block Grants: general purpose grants to state and local governments (but must comply with state or local rules)
- Items that would directly reduce the cost of carrying out the grant
- Legislation that would cause "material impairment" of the groups' ability or authority to carry out the grant
- Advocating changes in administrative regulations of federal agencies
- Providing information and assistance to legislators or their staff at their request if:
    1. The request is specific
    2. The request is directed to the group or the general public
    3. You respond only to the requestor
    4. Presentations can be in writing or oral, but must be mostly informational
    5. Presentation related directly to performance of the grant
    6. The information must be readily obtainable

Source: OMB Circular A-122

# Five Tips for Nonprofit Leaders Interested in Advocacy

Nonprofit advocacy may be motivated by moral, ethical, or faith principles, by the people served or issues addressed. Some nonprofits respond to attacks on their organization or issue area, or to protect an asset, such as funding. In all cases, engaging in policy advocacy can help the organization move closer to accomplishing its mission.

And yet, according to the Center for Responsive Politics, nonprofits are less likely to engage in advocacy. For example, at the federal level, in 2009, 422 nonprofits spent $42.6 million and employed 1,005 lobbyists. By comparison, business associations, the second largest industry, dwarfed nonprofit lobbying with $183.1 million spent.

Advocacy is like exercise. Do it regularly, it becomes part of daily life, and your organization will be healthier; plus, it rubs off on others. Do it irregularly, it is uncomfortable, and doing a lot quickly can hurt. This may be why groups that suddenly jump into advocacy when they are under attack – stop when the attack is over. They aren't in shape, and it seems hard. So, if your organization is new to advocacy, plan to start slowly and build your civic engagement muscles. Here are five useful steps to get started.

## 1. Create an environment where advocacy can flourish.

Everyone - executive director, board members, and staff - must demonstrate strong, consistent support for engaging in advocacy.

Three steps are key: *discuss, reward,* and *act.* For example, in staff meetings, is there discussion of advocacy issues? Are staff rewarded for engaging in advocacy? Is time made for advocacy actions? Are advocacy efforts noted in fundraising activities? Is the executive director comfortable with more than "safe" activities – like sending their newsletter to elected officials? Advocacy is a team sport, with a role for everyone.

The same goes for the board of directors. Is advocacy discussed at board meetings? Is there an advocacy or government affairs committee? Organizations with advocacy-related board committees are significantly more likely to engage in public policy matters – and with greater frequency. Helping board members to understand why advocacy is intrinsic to the organization's mission can create a legacy of organizational support for advocacy.

## 2. Establish procedures that make policy decision-making easier.

It is essential to have streamlined decision-making so the organization can quickly decide whether to act and, when needed, take quick action. Often, nonprofit groups have no clear procedures, or a very complex decision making process. For example, if the board has to approve all staff actions on policy matters, and only meets quarterly, key advocacy opportunities will be missed.

Some options: (a) the board sets broad policy direction, leaving it to the executive director to execute policy decisions that support the board's views; (b) a board committees agrees to meet via conference calls or via e-mail; and (c) board committees can be authorized to make decisions between board meetings. Whatever the arrangement, the mechanism needs to be clear to staff.

### 3. Make sure at least one person in the organization has advocacy responsibility – someone other than the executive director.

Assigning public policy responsibility to at least one person in an organization significantly increases the likelihood of engagement in public policy. This responsibility should be built into the person's job description and be well-known to others. Organizations that assign public policy responsibilities to someone other than the executive direct (e.g., a lobbyist outside the organization, other staff members, board committees, volunteers), are more likely to lobby and testify - and more consistently. (The executive director typically pushes public policy advocacy to the back burner.)

### 4. Belong to Associations that can represent you before government.

Joining an association that speaks out on public policy issues gives you a louder voice, and is linked to whether an organization engages in public policy. Those joining state and/or national associations engage in more direct lobbying, indirect lobbying, and testifying, and they do so with greater frequency. Nonprofit budgets should identify funds for dues to associations that engage in public policy.

### 5. Get training.

It's been noted that advocacy is like exercise. If it were like riding a bike, most would agree it is easy, but the first time can be hard. Thus, the best step is to get training and technical support; happily, these days many resources exist. Here are four areas where training and technical assistance might prove useful.

- **Organizational capacity building.** Nonprofits often need help to create the right type of organizational structure (e.g., board role, staff responsibilities) to engage in advocacy. Today, state/local nonprofit associations and many management consultants can help.

- **How to advocate and lobby effectively.** Here too, many services and consultants exist to help nonprofits be effective advocates. For example, many state nonprofit associations have useful websites and offer excellent trainings. Other websites, such as OMB Watch's NPAction.org and the Nonprofit Good Practice Guide (www.npgoodpractice.org) are also useful. There are excellent books and guides, such as Marcia Avner's *Lobbying and Advocacy Handbook for Nonprofit Organizations: Shaping Public Policy at the State and Local Level* or Nancy Amidei's *So You Want To Make a Difference* (available through OMB Watch). There are also materials for media and communications strategies now readily available, such as *Strategic Communications for Nonprofits: A Step-by-Step Guide to Working with the Media* by Kathy Bonk, Emily Tynes, Henry Griggs and Phil Sparks.

- **Training on civics and policymaking.** Being an effective advocate means knowing the basics of how policymaking works. Here too, nonprofit associations can get help with basic civics lesson refreshers, including how to monitor and comment on regulations.

- **Training on laws and regulations governing nonprofits.** For this, turn to two excellent resources: the Alliance for Justice (afj.org), and the Center for Lobbying in the Public Interest (CLPI.org). Both offer materials, consultation, and trainings.

Adapted from: *Seen but not Heard: Strengthening Nonprofit Advocacy* by Gary D. Bass, David F. Arons, Kay Guinane, & Matthew Carter

1742 Connecticut Avenue, NW  Washington, DC 20009
PHONE: (202) 234-8494   FAX: (202) 234-8584
www.ombwatch.org
ombwatch@ombwatch.org

Made in the USA
Monee, IL
18 April 2020